Teach Yourself VISUALLY™
Access 2002

Visual™

From
maranGraphics®

&

Wiley Publishing, Inc.

Teach Yourself VISUALLY™ Access 2002

Published by
Wiley Publishing, Inc.
909 Third Avenue
New York, NY 10022

Published simultaneously in Canada

Copyright©2002 by maranGraphics Inc.
 5755 Coopers Avenue
 Mississauga, Ontario, Canada
 L4Z 1R9

Library of Congress Control Number: 2002100391

ISBN: 0-7645-3591-9

Manufactured in the United States of America

10 9 8 7 6 5 4 3

1K/QR/RQ/QS/MG

Trademark Acknowledgments

Important Numbers

For U.S. corporate orders, please call maranGraphics at 800-469-6616 or fax 905-890-9434.

For general information on our other products and services or to obtain technical support, please contact our Customer Care Department within the U.S. at 800-762-2974, outside the U.S. at 317-572-3993 or fax 317-572-4002.

Permissions

Wiley Publishing, Inc.   is a trademark of
                          Wiley Publishing, Inc.

U.S. Corporate Sales	**U.S. Trade Sales**
Contact maranGraphics at (800) 469-6616 or fax (905) 890-9434.	Contact Wiley at (800) 762-2974 or fax (317) 572-4002.

Some comments from our readers...

"I have to praise you and your company on the fine products you turn out. I have twelve of the *Teach Yourself VISUALLY* and *Simplified* books in my house. They were instrumental in helping me pass a difficult computer course. Thank you for creating books that are easy to follow."

–Gordon Justin (Brielle, NJ)

"I commend your efforts and your success. I teach in an outreach program for the Dr. Eugene Clark Library in Lockhart, TX. Your *Teach Yourself VISUALLY* books are incredible and I use them in my computer classes. All my students love them!"

–Michele Schalin (Lockhart, TX)

"Thank you so much for helping people like me learn about computers. The Maran family is just what the doctor ordered. Thank you, thank you, thank you."

–Carol Moten (New Kensington, PA)

"I would like to take this time to compliment maranGraphics on creating such great books. Thank you for making it clear. Keep up the good work."

–Kirk Santoro (Burbank, CA)

"I write to extend my thanks and appreciation for your books. They are clear, easy to follow, and straight to the point. Keep up the good work!"

–Seward Kollie (Dakar, Senegal)

"What fantastic teaching books you have produced! Congratulations to you and your staff. You deserve the Nobel prize in Education in the Software category. Thanks for helping me to understand computers."

–Bruno Tonon (Melbourne, Australia)

"Over time, I have bought a number of your 'Read Less-Learn More' books. For me, they are THE way to learn anything easily."

–José A. Mazón (Cuba, NY)

"I was introduced to maranGraphics about four years ago and YOU ARE THE GREATEST THING THAT EVER HAPPENED TO INTRODUCTORY COMPUTER BOOKS!"

–Glenn Nettleton (Huntsville, AL)

"Compliments To The Chef!! Your books are extraordinary! Or, simply put, Extra-Ordinary, meaning way above the rest! THANK YOU THANK YOU THANK YOU! for creating these."

–Christine J. Manfrin (Castle Rock, CO)

"I'm a grandma who was pushed by an 11-year-old grandson to join the computer age. I found myself hopelessly confused and frustrated until I discovered the Visual series. I'm no expert by any means now, but I'm a lot further along than I would have been otherwise. Thank you!"

–Carol Louthain (Logansport, IN)

"Thank you, thank you, thank you...for making it so easy for me to break into this high-tech world. I now own four of your books. I recommend them to anyone who is a beginner like myself. Now... if you could just do one for programming VCRs, it would make my day!"

–Gay O'Donnell (Calgary, Alberta, Canada)

"You're marvelous! I am greatly in your debt."

–Patrick Baird (Lacey, WA)

maranGraphics is a family-run business
located near Toronto, Canada.

At **maranGraphics**, we believe in producing great computer books–one book at a time.

Each maranGraphics book uses the award-winning communication process that we have been developing over the last 25 years. Using this process, we organize screen shots, text and illustrations in a way that makes it easy for you to learn new concepts and tasks.

We spend hours deciding the best way to perform each task, so you don't have to! Our clear, easy-to-follow screen shots and instructions walk you through each task from beginning to end.

Our detailed illustrations go hand-in-hand with the text to help reinforce the information. Each illustration is a labor of love–some take up to a week to draw!

We want to thank you for purchasing what we feel are the best computer books money can buy. We hope you enjoy using this book as much as we enjoyed creating it!

Sincerely,

The Maran Family

Please visit us on the Web at:

www.maran.com

CREDITS

Author:
Ruth Maran

Copy Developer:
Raquel Scott

Technical Consultant:
Paul Whitehead

Project Manager:
Judy Maran

**Editing and
Screen Captures:**
Roderick Anatalio
Norm Schumacher
Megan Kirby

Layout Artist:
Treena Lees

Illustrators:
Russ Marini
Steven Schaerer

Screen Artist and Illustrator:
Darryl Grossi

Indexer:
Raquel Scott

Permissions Coordinator:
Jennifer Amaral

**Wiley Vice President and
Executive Group Publisher:**
Richard Swadley

**Wiley Vice President
and Publisher:**
Barry Pruett

Wiley Editorial Support:
Jennifer Dorsey
Sandy Rodrigues
Lindsay Sandman

Post Production:
Robert Maran

ACKNOWLEDGMENTS

Thanks to the dedicated staff of maranGraphics, including
Jennifer Amaral, Roderick Anatalio, Darryl Grossi,
Kelleigh Johnson, Megan Kirby, Wanda Lawrie, Treena Lees,
Cathy Lo, Jill Maran, Judy Maran, Robert Maran, Ruth Maran,
Russ Marini, Steven Schaerer, Norm Schumacher, Raquel Scott,
Roxanne Van Damme and Paul Whitehead.

Finally, to Richard Maran who originated the easy-to-use graphic
format of this guide. Thank you for your inspiration and guidance.

TABLE OF CONTENTS

Chapter 1

GETTING STARTED

Chapter 2

CREATE TABLES

Chapter 3

Chapter 4

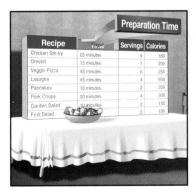

TABLE OF CONTENTS

Chapter 5

ESTABLISH RELATIONSHIPS

Chapter 6

CREATE FORMS

Chapter 7

DESIGN FORMS

Chapter 8

Chapter 9

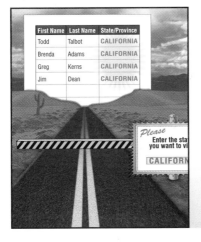

TABLE OF CONTENTS

Chapter 10

USING THE PIVOTTABLE AND PIVOTCHART VIEWS

Chapter 11

CREATE REPORTS

Chapter 12

PRINT INFORMATION

Chapter 13

CREATE DATA ACCESS PAGES

Getting Started

Are you ready to begin using Microsoft Access 2002? This chapter will help you get started.

INTRODUCTION TO ACCESS

Microsoft® Access is a database program that allows you to store and manage large collections of information. Access provides you with all the tools you need to create an efficient and effective database.

Many individuals use databases to store personal information such as addresses, music collections, recipes and wine lists.

Companies use databases to store information such as mailing lists, client orders, expenses, inventory and payroll.

DATABASE APPLICATIONS

Store Information

A database stores and manages a collection of information related to a particular subject or purpose. You can efficiently review, add, update and organize the information stored in a database.

Find Information

You can instantly locate information of interest in a database. For example, you can find all clients with the last name "Smith." You can also perform more advanced searches, such as finding all clients living in California who purchased more than $1,000 of your products last year.

Analyze and Print Information

You can perform calculations on the information in a database to help you make quick, accurate and informed decisions. You can neatly present the information in professionally designed reports.

USING THE MOUSE

A mouse is a handheld device that allows you to select and move items on your screen.

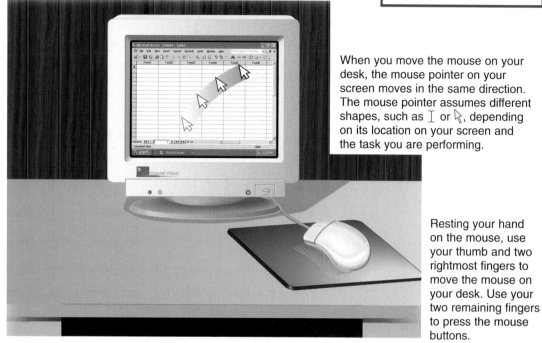

When you move the mouse on your desk, the mouse pointer on your screen moves in the same direction. The mouse pointer assumes different shapes, such as I or $\mathbb{k}$, depending on its location on your screen and the task you are performing.

Resting your hand on the mouse, use your thumb and two rightmost fingers to move the mouse on your desk. Use your two remaining fingers to press the mouse buttons.

MOUSE ACTIONS

Click

Press and release the left mouse button. A click is usually used to select an item on the screen.

Double-click

Quickly press and release the left mouse button twice. A double-click is usually used to open an item.

Right-click

Press and release the right mouse button. A right-click is usually used to display a list of frequently used commands for an item.

Drag

Position the mouse pointer over an item on your screen and then press and hold down the left mouse button as you move the mouse to where you want to place the item. Then release the mouse button.

START ACCESS

You can start Access to create a new database or work with a database you previously created.

1 Click **start** to display the Start menu.

2 Click **All Programs** to view a list of the programs on your computer.

3 Click **Microsoft Access**.

■ The Microsoft Access window appears.

■ The task pane appears each time you start Access, allowing you to quickly perform common tasks.

■ A button for Microsoft Access appears on the taskbar.

EXIT ACCESS

When you finish
using Access,
you can exit the
program.

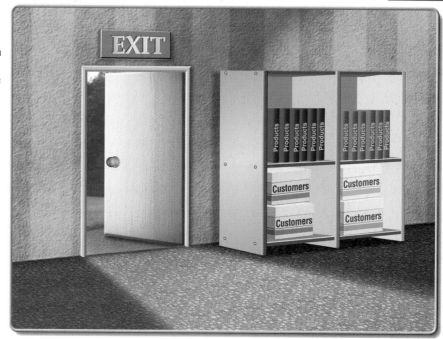

You should always
exit Access and all
other programs
before turning off
your computer.

EXIT ACCESS

■ Before exiting Access,
you should save and close
all open objects in your
database, such as a form
or report.

1 Click **File**.

2 Click **Exit**.

*Note: If Exit does not appear
on the menu, position the
mouse ▷ over the bottom
of the menu to display the
option.*

■ The Microsoft Access
window disappears from
your screen.

■ The button for the
Microsoft Access window
disappears from the
taskbar.

PARTS OF A DATABASE

A database consists of objects such as tables, forms, queries, reports and pages.

Tables

A table stores a collection of information about a specific topic, such as a mailing list. You can have one or more tables in a database. A table consists of fields and records.

Address ID	First Name	Last Name	Address	City	State/Province	Postal Code
1	Jim	Schmith	258 Linton Ave.	New York	NY	10010
2	Brenda	Petterson	50 Tree Lane	Boston	MA	02117
3	Todd	Talbot	68 Cracker Ave.	San Francisco	CA	94110
4	Chuck	Dean	47 Crosby Ave.	Las Vegas	NV	89116
5	Melanie	Robinson	26 Arnold Cres.	Jacksonville	FL	32256
6	Susan	Hughes	401 Idon Dr.	Nashville	TN	37243
7	Allen	Toppins	10 Heldon St.	Atlanta	GA	30375
8	Greg	Kilkenny	36 Buzzard St.	Boston	MA	02118
9	Jason	Marcuson	15 Bizzo Pl.	New York	NY	10020
10	Jim	Martin	890 Apple St.	San Diego	CA	92121

Field

A field is a specific category of information in a table, such as the first names of all your customers.

Record

A record is a collection of information about one person, place or thing in a table, such as the name and address of one customer.

Forms

Forms provide a quick way to view, enter and edit information in a database by presenting information in an attractive, easy-to-use format. Forms display boxes that clearly show you where to enter and/or edit information. Forms usually display one record at a time.

Queries

Queries allow you to find information of interest in a database. You can enter criteria in a query to specify what information you want to find. For example, you can create a query to find every customer who lives in California.

Reports

Reports are professional-looking documents that summarize information from a database. You can perform calculations in a report to help you analyze the data. For example, you can create a report that displays the total sales for each product.

Pages

Data access pages are Web pages that connect directly to the information in your database. You can use these pages to view, enter, edit and analyze data in your database from the Internet or your company's intranet.

PLAN A DATABASE

You should take the time to plan your database. A well-planned database helps ensure that you will be able to perform tasks efficiently and accurately.

Determine the Purpose of Your Database

Decide what information you want your database to store and how you plan to use the information. If colleagues, friends or family members will use the database, you should consult with them to determine how they plan to use the database.

Determine the Tables You Need

Gather all the information you want to store in your database and then divide the information into separate tables. Each table should contain information for only one subject, such as a list of customer addresses.

The same information should not appear in more than one table in your database. You can work more efficiently and reduce errors if you only need to update information in one table.

Determine the Fields You Need

A field is a specific category of information in a table, such as the last name of every client.

➤ Each field should relate directly to the subject of a table.

➤ Make sure you break information in a table into its smallest parts. For example, break down names into two fields called First Name and Last Name.

➤ Try to keep the number of fields in a table to a minimum. Tables with many fields increase the time Access takes to process information.

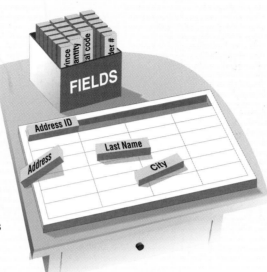

➤ Do not include a field that contains data you can calculate using other fields. For example, if a table includes a Unit Price field and a Quantity field, do not include a field that multiplies the values in these two fields. Access can perform the calculations for you and will update the calculations each time you change values in the fields.

Determine the Primary Key in Each Table

Each table in your database should have a primary key. A primary key is one or more fields that uniquely identifies each record in a table. For example, the primary key in a table containing employee information can be the social security number for each employee.

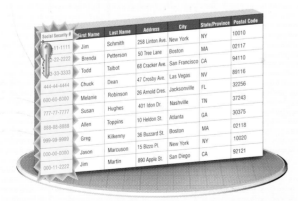

Determine the Relationships Between Tables

Relationships between tables allow Access to bring together related information stored in separate tables in your database. For example, you can create a relationship between the Customers table and the Orders table. You usually relate the primary key in one table to a matching field in another table to create a relationship.

CREATE A DATABASE USING THE DATABASE WIZARD

You can use the Database Wizard to quickly and easily create a database. The wizard saves you time by creating the tables, forms, queries and reports for your database.

You can use the Database Wizard to create many types of databases, such as databases for contact management, expenses, inventory control and order entry.

You can have only one database open at a time. Access will close a database displayed on your screen when you create a new database.

CREATE A DATABASE USING THE DATABASE WIZARD

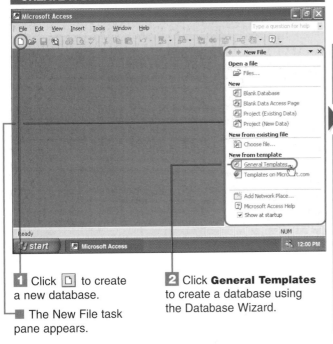

1 Click ⬜ to create a new database.

■ The New File task pane appears.

2 Click **General Templates** to create a database using the Database Wizard.

■ The Templates dialog box appears.

3 Click the **Databases** tab.

4 Click the database template that best describes the type of database you want to create.

5 Click **OK** to create the database.

■ The File New Database dialog box appears.

How can I quickly select a database template I recently used?

The New File task pane displays the names of the last two database templates you used. To display the New File task pane, perform step 1 on page 12.

1 To select a database template you recently used, click the name of the template.

How can I get more database templates?

When you are connected to the Internet, click **Templates on Microsoft.com** on the New File task pane. To display the New File task pane, perform step 1 on page 12. A Web page will appear, allowing you to obtain more database templates that you can use.

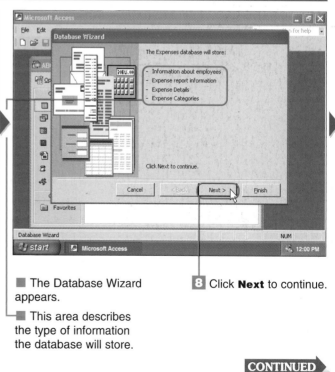

6 Type a name for your database.

■ This area shows the location where Access will store your database. You can click this area to change the location.

■ This area allows you to access commonly used locations. To access a commonly used location, click the location.

7 Click **Create** to create the database.

■ The Database Wizard appears.

■ This area describes the type of information the database will store.

8 Click **Next** to continue.

CONTINUED

The Database Wizard displays the fields that each table in your database will include. You can choose to include additional fields in each table.

A field is a specific category of information in a table, such as the last names of all your customers.

CREATE A DATABASE USING THE DATABASE WIZARD (CONTINUED)

■ This area displays the tables Access will include in your database.

9 Click a table to display the fields in the table.

■ This area displays the fields in the table you selected. The fields displaying a check mark (✔) are required fields and must be included in the table. The fields shown in *italics* are optional.

10 To add an optional field to the table, click the box (☐) beside the field (☐ changes to ☑). Repeat this step for each optional field you want to include in the table.

■ To add optional fields to other tables in the database, repeat steps **9** and **10** for each table.

11 Click **Next** to continue.

**Can I remove a required field from
a table in the Database Wizard?**

No. You can remove a required
field from a table only after you
finish creating the database.
When you try to remove a required
field in the Database Wizard, a
message will appear, stating that
the field is required and must be
selected. To remove a field from
a table after you finish creating
the database, see page 45.

12 Click the style you want
to use for screen displays.

■ This area displays a
sample of the style you
selected.

13 Click **Next** to continue.

■ You can click **Back**
at any time to return to a
previous step and change
your selections.

14 Click the style you
want to use for printed
reports.

■ This area displays a
sample of the style you
selected.

15 Click **Next** to continue.

CONTINUED

CREATE A DATABASE USING THE DATABASE WIZARD

When the Database Wizard finishes creating your database, Access displays a switchboard that you can use to perform common tasks in the database.

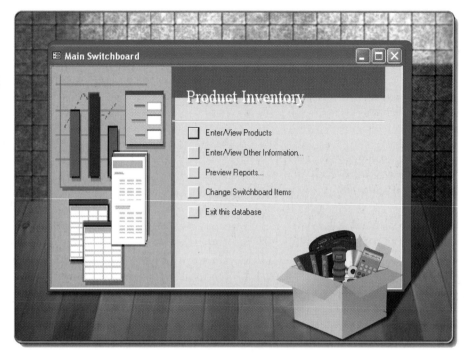

A switchboard is a menu that offers a list of choices.

CREATE A DATABASE USING THE DATABASE WIZARD (CONTINUED)

16 This area displays the title of your database. To use a different title, type the title.

17 Click **Next** to continue.

■ The Database Wizard indicates that you have provided all the information needed to create your database.

18 Click **Finish** to create your database.

Why does this dialog box appear when I finish using the Database Wizard?

Access needs you to enter information, such as your company name and address, to finish setting up the database.

■ To close the dialog box and display a form that provides areas for you to enter your information, click **OK**. To enter data into a form, see page 144.

Do I have to use the Main Switchboard to work with my database?

No. Instead of using the Main Switchboard window, you can use the Database window to work with your database. To quickly display the Database window at any time, press the **F11** key. For more information on the Database window, see page 24.

■ Access creates the objects for your database, including tables, forms, queries and reports.

■ The Main Switchboard window appears, displaying options you can select to perform common tasks in the database.

19 To perform a task, click the task you want to perform.

■ The database object that allows you to perform the task appears.

Note: If a list of additional tasks appears, repeat step 19 to select the task you want to perform.

20 When you finish using the database object, click ✕ to close the object and return to the switchboard.

CREATE A BLANK DATABASE

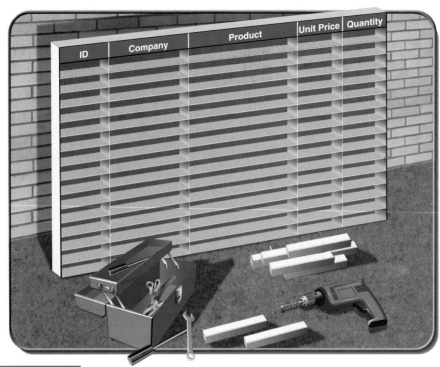

If you want to design your own database, you can create a blank database. Creating a blank database gives you the most flexibility and control when designing a database.

You can have only one database open at a time. Access will close a database displayed on your screen when you create or open another database.

CREATE A BLANK DATABASE

1 Click 🗋 to create a blank database.

■ The New File task pane appears.

2 Click **Blank Database** to create a blank database.

■ The File New Database dialog box appears.

3 Type a name for your database.

**What are the commonly used locations I
can access when saving a blank database?**

History

Provides access to
folders and databases
you recently used.

My Documents

Provides a convenient
place to store a database.

Desktop

Allows you to store
a database on the
Windows desktop.

Favorites

Provides a place to
store a database you
will frequently use.

■ This area shows the
location where Access
will store your database.
You can click this area
to change the location.

■ This area allows you to
quickly access commonly
used locations. To access
a commonly used location,
click the location.

4 Click **Create** to create
the database.

■ Access creates a blank
database.

■ The Database window
appears. This window
allows you to create and
work with objects in your
database, such as tables,
queries and reports.

■ This area displays the
name of the database.

OPEN A DATABASE

You can open a database to view the database on your screen. Opening a database allows you to review and make changes to the database.

You can have only one database open at a time. Access will close a database displayed on your screen when you open another database.

OPEN A DATABASE

1 Click 🗁 to open a database.

■ The Open dialog box appears.

■ This area shows the location of the displayed databases. You can click this area to change the location.

■ This area allows you to access databases in commonly used locations. You can click a location to display the databases in the location.

Note: For information on the commonly used locations, see the top of page 19.

How can I quickly open a database I recently used?

Access remembers the names of the last four databases you used. You can use the New File task pane to quickly open any of these databases. The New File task pane appears each time you start Access.

1 To quickly open a database, click the name of the database you want to open.

Note: If the New File task pane is not displayed, click □ to display the task pane.

2 Click the name of the database you want to open.

3 Click **Open** to open the database.

■ The database opens and appears on your screen. You can now review and make changes to the database.

SEARCH FOR A DATABASE

If you cannot find
a database you
want to work with,
you can search for
the database.

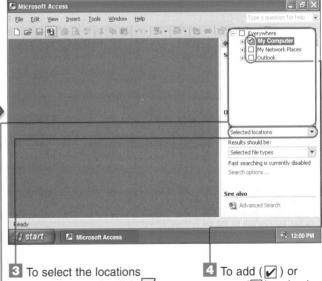

1 Click 🔍 to search
for a database.

■ The Basic Search
task pane appears.

2 Click this area and
type all or part of the name
of the database you want
to find.

*Note: If the area already contains
text, drag the mouse I over the
existing text and then type all or
part of the database name.*

3 To select the locations
you want to search, click ▼
in this area.

■ A check mark (✓)
appears beside each location
that Access will search.

*Note: By default, Access will search
all the drives and folders on your
computer.*

4 To add (✓) or
remove (☐) a check
mark, click the box
beside a location.

5 To close the list of
locations, click outside
the list.

22

When selecting the locations I want to search, how can I display more locations?

Each location that displays a plus sign (⊞) contains hidden locations. To display hidden locations, click the plus sign (⊞) beside a location (⊞ changes to ⊟). To once again hide the locations, click the minus sign (⊟) beside a location.

Can I view information about the databases that Access found?

Yes. To view information about a database that Access found, position the mouse 🖑 over the database. A yellow box will appear, displaying the location of the database and the date you last made changes to the database.

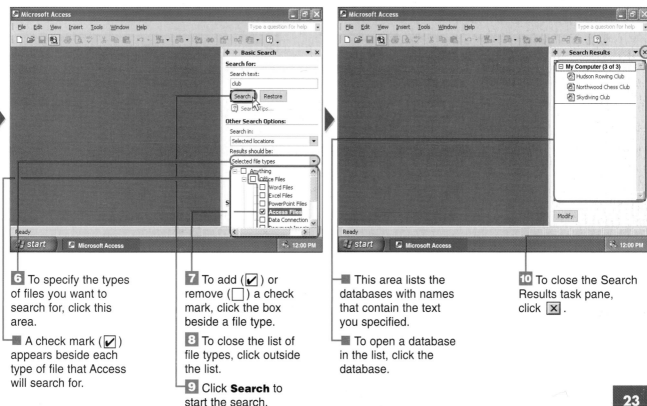

6 To specify the types of files you want to search for, click this area.

■ A check mark (☑) appears beside each type of file that Access will search for.

7 To add (☑) or remove (☐) a check mark, click the box beside a file type.

8 To close the list of file types, click outside the list.

9 Click **Search** to start the search.

■ This area lists the databases with names that contain the text you specified.

■ To open a database in the list, click the database.

10 To close the Search Results task pane, click ☒.

USING THE DATABASE WINDOW

You can use the Database window to open and work with objects in your database, such as tables, queries, forms, reports and pages.

USING THE DATABASE WINDOW

■ Each table, query, form, report and data access page in your database appears in the Database window.

■ If the Database window is hidden behind other windows, press the **F11** key to display the Database window.

■ This area displays the types of objects in your database.

1 Click the type of object you want to work with.

■ This area displays all the objects of the type you selected.

2 To open an object, double-click the object.

24

What types of objects will I find in the Database window?

Tables

Tables store information about a specific topic, such as a mailing list.

Queries

Queries allow you to find information of interest in your database.

Forms

Forms provide a quick way to view, enter and edit data in your database.

Reports

Reports summarize and print the data from your database in professional-looking documents.

Pages

Data access pages allow you to view, enter, edit and analyze data in your database from the Internet or your company's intranet.

■ The object opens and appears on your screen.

3 When you finish working with the object, click ✕ to close the object and return to the Database window.

CHANGE APPEARANCE OF OBJECTS

1 To change the appearance of the objects in the Database window, click one of the following buttons.

⬚ Large Icons

⬚ Small Icons

⬚ List

⬚ Details

MINIMIZE A WINDOW

If you are not using a window, you can minimize the window to temporarily remove it from your screen. You can redisplay the window at any time.

Minimizing a window allows you to temporarily put a window aside so you can work on another task.

MINIMIZE A WINDOW

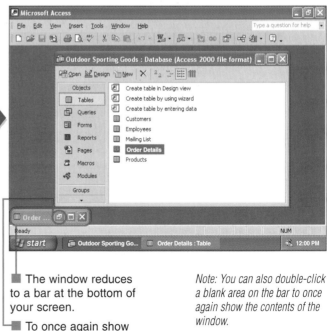

1 Click ▬ in the window you want to minimize.

■ The window reduces to a bar at the bottom of your screen.

■ To once again show the contents of the window, click 🗗 to restore the window to its original size.

Note: You can also double-click a blank area on the bar to once again show the contents of the window.

DISPLAY OR HIDE A TOOLBAR

Access offers several toolbars that you can display or hide at any time. Each toolbar contains buttons that you can use to perform common tasks.

The available toolbars depend on the task you are performing.

DISPLAY OR HIDE A TOOLBAR

1 Click **View**.

2 Click **Toolbars**.

■ A list of toolbars appears. A check mark (✔) beside the name of a toolbar indicates that the toolbar is currently displayed.

Note: The Task Pane also appears in the list of toolbars. Like a toolbar, the Task Pane allows you to perform common tasks.

3 Click the name of the toolbar you want to display or hide.

■ Access displays or hides the toolbar you selected.

GETTING HELP

If you do not know how to perform a task in Access, you can ask a question to find help information on the task.

1 Click this area and then type a question that explains the task you want to get help information on. Then press the **Enter** key.

■ A list of help topics related to your question appears.

2 Click a help topic of interest.

*Note: If more help topics exist, you can click **See more** to view the additional topics.*

28

What other ways can I obtain help?

In the Microsoft Access Help window, you can use the following tabs to obtain help information.

Index

You can type a word of interest and then press the Enter key or double-click a word in the alphabetical list of keywords to display help topics related to the word.

Contents

You can double-click a book icon (📖) or click a page icon (❓) to browse through the contents of Microsoft Access Help.

Answer Wizard

You can type a question and then press the Enter key to display help topics related to the question.

■ The Microsoft Access Help window appears.

Note: To maximize the Microsoft Access Help window to fill your screen, click 🔲 in the top right corner of the window.

■ This area displays the help topic you selected.

3 To display additional information for a word or phrase that appears in blue, click the word or phrase.

■ The additional information appears.

Note: The additional information may be a definition, a series of steps or a tip.

■ To once again hide the additional information, click the blue word or phrase.

4 When you finish reviewing the help information, click ✖ to close the Microsoft Access Help window.

Create Tables

Are you wondering how to create tables in your database? Learn how in this chapter.

CREATE A TABLE IN THE DATASHEET VIEW

You can create a
table to store new
information in
your database.

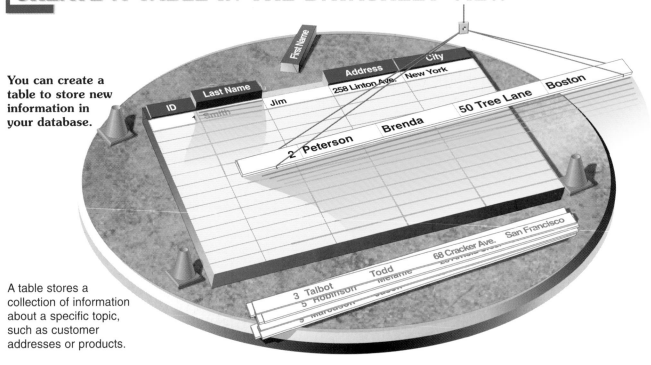

A table stores a
collection of information
about a specific topic,
such as customer
addresses or products.

CREATE A TABLE IN THE DATASHEET VIEW

1 Click **Tables** in the
Database window.

2 Double-click **Create
table by entering data**.

■ A blank table appears.

■ This area displays the
field name for each field
in your table.

3 To change a field name,
double-click the field name
to highlight the name.

What are the parts of a table?

Mailing List ID	First Name	Last Name	Address	City	State
1	Dan	Oberbroeckling	104 Sunset Ave.	Phoenix	AZ
2	Chuck	Deane	223 Beach St.	Denver	CO
3	Constance	Martin	27 Oak Dr.	Miami	FL
4	Kim	Grey	114 Jordan Dr.	Dallas	TX
5	Tim	Lampley	558 Colburg Rd.	Manhattan	NY
6	Kathleen	Matthews	48 Montana Ave	Little Rock	AR
7	Jeff	Davidson	89 Springhill Ave.	Chicago	IL
8	Jacqueline	Smith	6283 Main St.	Dallas	TX
9	Rev	Mengle	56 Palm St.	Columbus	OH
10	Jill	Proll	75 Ranch Blvd	Denver	CO
11	Mark	Harris	93 Crane St.	Phoenix	AZ
12	David	Gregory	4 Cherry Cres.	Miami	FL
13	Ronda	David-Burroughs	12 Mozart Dr.	Chicago	IL
(AutoNumber)					

Record: 1 of 13

Field Name

A field name identifies the information in a field.

Record

A record is a collection of information about one person, place or thing. For example, a record can contain a client's name and address.

Field

A field is a specific category of information and contains the same type of information for every record. For example, a field can contain the last name of every client.

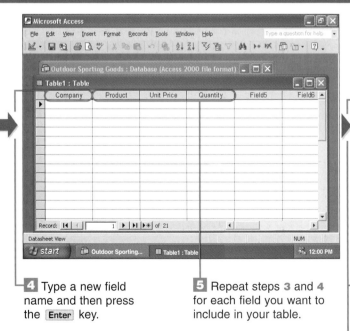

4 Type a new field name and then press the Enter key.

5 Repeat steps **3** and **4** for each field you want to include in your table.

6 To enter the data for a record, click the first empty cell in the table.

7 Type the data that corresponds to the field and then press the Enter key to move to the next field. Repeat this step until you finish entering all the data for the record.

8 Repeat steps **6** and **7** for each record you want to add to your table.

CONTINUED

CREATE A TABLE IN THE DATASHEET VIEW

When creating
a table, you
can have
Access create
a primary key
for the table.

Company ID	Company Name	Address	City	State/Province	Postal Code
1	Pet Superstore	258 Linton Ave.	New York	NY	10010
2	Petterson Inc.	50 Tree Lane	Boston	MA	02117
3	Martin Vet Supplies	68 Cracker Ave.	San Francisco	CA	94110
4	Greg's Pet Store	47 Crosby Ave.	Las Vegas	NV	89116
5	Pet Superstore	26 Arnold Cres.	Jacksonville	FL	32256
6	Feline Foods Inc.	401 Idon Dr.	Nashville	TN	37243
7	Weasels R Us	10 Heldon St.	Atlanta	GA	30375
8	Purrrfect Portions	36 Buzzard St.	Boston	MA	02118

A primary key
is one or more
fields that uniquely
identifies each
record in a table,
such as a field
containing ID
numbers. Each
table in your
database should
have a primary key.

CREATE A TABLE IN THE DATASHEET VIEW (CONTINUED)

9 Click 💾 to save your table.

■ The Save As dialog box appears.

10 Type a descriptive name for your table.

11 Click **OK** to save your table.

■ A dialog box appears, stating that your table does not have a primary key.

12 To have Access create a primary key for you, click **Yes**.

Note: If you have entered information that uniquely identifies each record, such as ID numbers or part numbers, you can click **No** to create your own primary key. To create or change a primary key, see page 122.

34

Why should each table in my database have a primary key?

Access uses the primary key in each table to establish relationships between the tables in your database. Relationships between tables allow Access to bring together related information in the tables. For more information on relationships, see page 124.

Will Access analyze the information I enter in a table?

When you save a table, Access analyzes the information you have entered and assigns a data type to each field. A data type determines the kind of information you can enter in a field, such as text, numbers or dates. For more information on data types, see page 82.

■ Access removes the rows and columns that do not contain data.

■ If you selected **Yes** in step **12**, Access adds an ID field to your table to serve as the primary key. The ID field automatically numbers each record in your table.

13 When you finish reviewing your records, click ☒ to close your table.

■ The name of your table appears in the Database window.

CREATE A TABLE USING THE TABLE WIZARD

You can use the Table Wizard to quickly create a table. The wizard asks you a series of questions and then sets up a table based on your answers.

The wizard can help you create a table for business or personal use. You can use the wizard to create tables such as Customers, Products, Orders, Recipes and Investments.

A table stores a collection of information about a specific topic, such as a mailing list.

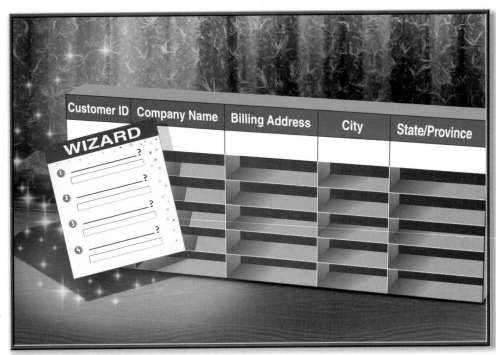

CREATE A TABLE USING THE TABLE WIZARD

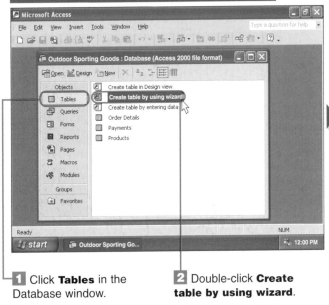

1 Click **Tables** in the Database window.

2 Double-click **Create table by using wizard**.

■ The Table Wizard appears.

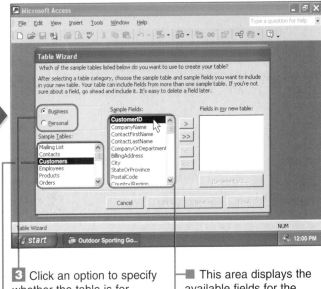

3 Click an option to specify whether the table is for business or personal use (○ changes to ⊙).

4 Click the sample table you want to use.

Note: The available sample tables depend on the option you selected in step 3.

■ This area displays the available fields for the sample table you selected.

5 Double-click each field you want to include in the table.

Note: To select all the fields at once, click >> .

What is a primary key?

A primary key is one or more fields that uniquely identifies each record in a table, such as a field containing ID numbers. Each table in your database should have a primary key. When using the Table Wizard to create a table, you can have Access set a primary key for you. Access will create a field that automatically numbers each record in your table. To later change the primary key, see page 122.

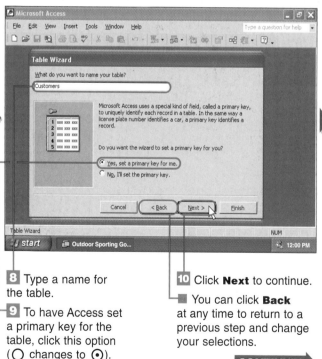

■ Each field you select appears in this area.

6 To remove a field you accidentally selected, double-click the field in this area.

Note: To remove all the fields you selected at once, click `<<`.

7 When you finish selecting all the fields you want to include in the table, click **Next** to continue.

8 Type a name for the table.

9 To have Access set a primary key for the table, click this option (○ changes to ⊙).

Note: For information on the primary key, see the top of this page.

10 Click **Next** to continue.

■ You can click **Back** at any time to return to a previous step and change your selections.

CONTINUED

CREATE A TABLE USING THE TABLE WIZARD

The Table Wizard shows how your new table relates to the other tables in your database.

Relationships between tables allow Access to bring together related information in the tables. For more information on relationships, see page 124.

CREATE A TABLE USING THE TABLE WIZARD (CONTINUED)

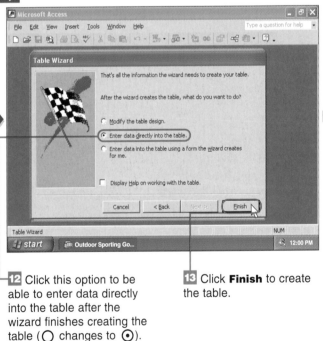

■ This screen appears if other tables exist in your database.

Note: If this screen does not appear, skip to step 12.

■ This area displays how the new table relates to the existing tables.

11 Click **Next** to continue.

12 Click this option to be able to enter data directly into the table after the wizard finishes creating the table (○ changes to ⊙).

13 Click **Finish** to create the table.

Can I make changes to a table?

Yes. After you create a table using the Table Wizard, you can make changes to the table. For example, you can change the width of columns, rename a field, rearrange fields, add a new field or delete a field. To make changes to a table, see pages 41 to 49.

Can I later add records to a table?

After you create a table, you can add new records to the table at any time. For example, you may want to add information about a new customer to a table containing customer information. To add new records to a table, see page 64.

■ This area displays the field names for the table.

■ If you selected **Yes** in step 9, Access adds an ID field to the table to serve as the primary key. The ID field will automatically number each record you add to the table.

14 To enter the data for a record, click the first empty cell in the table.

15 Type the data that corresponds to the field and then press the Enter key to move to the next field. Repeat this step until you finish entering all the data for the record.

16 Repeat steps **14** and **15** for each record you want to add to your table. Access automatically saves each record you enter.

17 When you finish entering records, click ✕ to close the table.

OPEN A TABLE

You can open a table to display its contents on your screen. Opening a table allows you to review and make changes to the table.

1 Click **Tables** in the Database window.

■ This area displays a list of the tables in your database.

2 Double-click the table you want to open.

■ The table opens. You can now review and make changes to the table.

■ When you finish working with the table, click ✕ to close the table.

*Note: A dialog box will appear if you did not save changes you made to the layout of the table. To specify if you want to save the changes, click **Yes** or **No**.*

You can change
the width of a
column in a table.
Increasing the
width of a column
allows you to view
data that is too
long to display
in the column.

Reducing
the width of
columns allows
you to display
more fields on
your screen at
once.

CHANGE A COLUMN WIDTH

1 To change the width of a
column, position the mouse I
over the right edge of the
column heading (I changes
to ↔).

2 Drag the column edge
until the line displays the
column width you want.

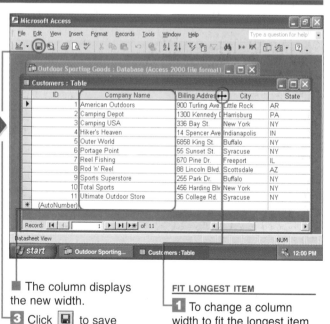

■ The column displays
the new width.

3 Click 🖫 to save
your change.

FIT LONGEST ITEM

1 To change a column
width to fit the longest item
in the column, double-click
the right edge of the column
heading.

RENAME A FIELD

You can give a field a new name to more accurately describe the contents of the field.

RECIPES Table

Recipe ID	Recipe Name	Time	Meal	Servings
1	Chicken Stir-fry	25 minutes	Dinner	4
2	Omelet	15 minutes	Breakfast	1
3	Veggie Pizza	45 minutes	Lunch	6
	Lasagna	45 minutes	Dinner	
		10 minutes	Breakf...	

Preparation Time

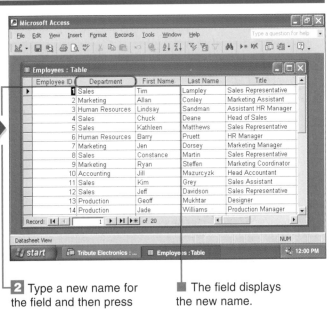

1 Double-click the field name you want to change.

■ The field name is highlighted.

2 Type a new name for the field and then press the Enter key.

■ The field displays the new name.

42

You can change
the order of
fields to better
organize the
information in
a table.

Rearranging fields in
the Datasheet view
will not affect how
the fields appear in
the Design view of a
table. For information
on the views of a
table, see page 74.

REARRANGE FIELDS

1 Click the name of the
field you want to move.
The field is highlighted.

2 Position the mouse
over the field name and
then drag the field to a
new location.

■ A thick line shows
where the field will appear.

■ The field appears
in the new location.

3 Click 🖫 to save
your change.

ADD A FIELD

You can add a field to a table when you want the table to include an additional category of information.

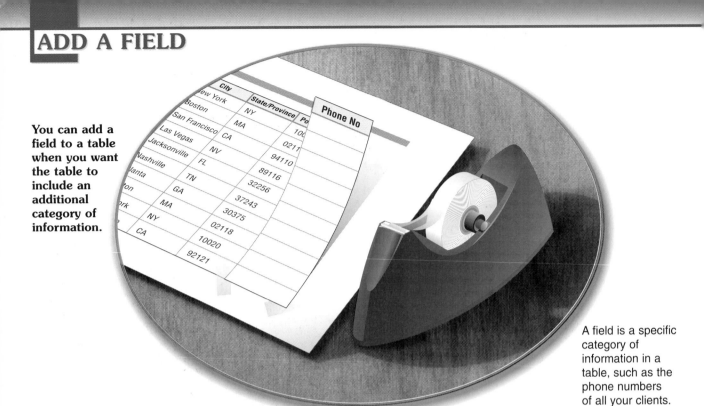

A field is a specific category of information in a table, such as the phone numbers of all your clients.

ADD A FIELD

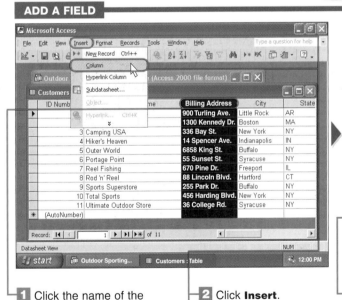

1 Click the name of the field you want to appear after the new field. The field is highlighted.

2 Click **Insert**.

3 Click **Column**.

■ The new field appears in your table.

■ Access assigns a name to the new field. To give the field a descriptive name, see page 42 to rename the field.

DELETE A FIELD

**If you no longer
need a field, you
can permanently
delete the field
from a table.**

Before you delete a
field, make sure the
field is not used in
any other objects in
your database, such as
a form, query or report.

You cannot delete a field
used to create a relationship
to another table in the
database. For information
on relationships, see page 124.

DELETE A FIELD

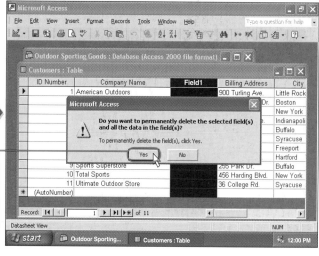

1 Click the name of the
field you want to delete.
The field is highlighted.

2 Click **Edit**.

3 Click **Delete Column**.

■ A confirmation dialog box
appears.

4 Click **Yes** to permanently
delete the field.

■ The field disappears
from your table.

45

CHANGE THE APPEARANCE OF A TABLE

You can change the cell style and colors in a table to enhance the appearance of the table.

■1 Click **Format**.

■2 Click **Datasheet**.

■ The Datasheet Formatting dialog box appears.

■3 Click the cell effect you want to use (○ changes to ⊙).

*Note: If you selected **Raised** or **Sunken** in step 3, skip to step 9.*

■4 To remove the horizontal or vertical gridlines, click each gridline you want to remove (☑ changes to ☐).

■5 To change the background color, click this area to display a list of the available colors.

■6 Click the background color you want to use.

How can I change the border or line styles in a table?

In the Datasheet Formatting dialog box, you can change the border and line styles in a table.

■ You can click this area to select the type of border or line you want to change.

■ You can click this area to select a style for the type of border or line you selected.

Can I change the appearance of a form or query?

You can also perform the steps shown below to change the appearance of a form or a query displayed in the Datasheet view. To change the view of a form or query, see page 150 or 200.

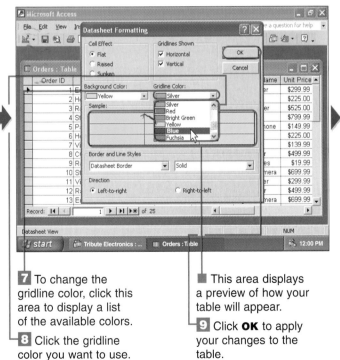

7 To change the gridline color, click this area to display a list of the available colors.

8 Click the gridline color you want to use.

■ This area displays a preview of how your table will appear.

9 Click **OK** to apply your changes to the table.

■ The table displays the changes you selected.

10 Click 🖫 to save your changes.

RENAME A TABLE

You can change the name of a table to better describe the information stored in the table.

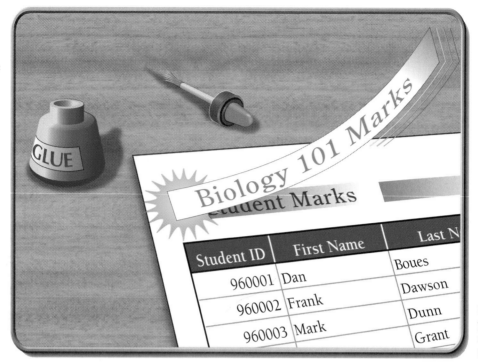

Each table in your database must have a unique name.

RENAME A TABLE

1 Click **Tables** in the Database window.

■ This area displays a list of the tables in your database.

2 Click the name of the table you want to rename.

3 After a few seconds, click the name again or press the **F2** key. A black border appears around the name.

Note: If you accidentally double-click the name of the table, the table will open.

4 Type a new name for the table and then press the **Enter** key.

■ The table displays the new name.

DELETE A TABLE

If you no longer need the information stored in a table, you can permanently delete the table from your database.

Before you delete a table, make sure the table is not used by other objects in your database, such as a form, query or report.

You cannot delete a table that is related to another table in your database. For information on relationships, see page 124.

DELETE A TABLE

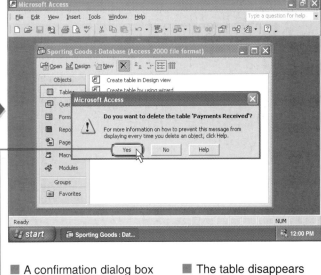

1 Click **Tables** in the Database window.

■ This area displays a list of the tables in your database.

2 Click the name of the table you want to delete.

3 Click ☒ to delete the table.

■ A confirmation dialog box appears.

4 Click **Yes** to permanently delete the table.

■ The table disappears from the Database window.

49

Book ID	Title	Year P...
1	*Spaceships in Orbit*	
2	*Escape from Reality*	
3	*Hugh's Haunted Castle*	
4	*Still Waters Run Deep*	
5	*The Tourist*	
6	*The Cowboy Invasion*	
7	*My Clandestine Ways*	
8	*The Magical Lilac Tree*	

Customers

Customer ID	First Name	Last Name	Phone Number	Fax Number
1064	Carol	Barclay	(201) 555-4591	(201) 555-1264
5469	Mark	Dunn	(201) 555-1278	(201) 555-1287
3570	Peter	Lejcar	(201) 555-1975	(201) 555-1064
2146	Tim	Matthews	(201) 555-1946	(201) 555-1953
7521	Deborah	Peterson	(201) 555-1976	(201) 555-1967
2368	John	Smith	(201) 555-1944	(201) 555-1994
3494	Tina	Veltri	(201) 555-	(201) 555-1424
7321	Frank	Dawson	(201) 555-1479	(201) 555-1462

Edit Tables

Do you want to work with and edit the data in your tables? This chapter teaches you how to add and remove records, hide and freeze fields in your tables and more.

ORDERS Table

Order ID	Company Name	Product	Quantity	Unit Price
1	Pet Superstore	Vitamins	12	$20.00
2	Petterson Inc.	Bulk Dry Food	15	$18.00
3	Martin Vet Supplies	Diet Dog Food	20	$12.00
4	Greg's Pet Store	5-Variety Biscuits	50	$8.50
5	Pet Superstore	Canned Dog Food	54	$3.00
6	Feline Foods Inc.	Dry Cat Food	40	$4.00
7	Weasels R Us	Ferret Pellets	20	$6.50
8	Purrrfect Portions	Dry Cat Food	54	$4.00
9	Doggone Yummy Inc.	Steak-flavored Bones	40	$1.25
10	Jim's Pets	Hamster Treats	30	$5.50
11	Allen's Dog Kennel	Puppy Kibble	20	$8.50
12	B&T Food Suppliers	Gerbil Mix	25	$4.50
13	Pet Superstore	Parrot Food	25	$17.00
14	Kitty-Mart	Dry Cat Food	35	$4.00
15	Canine Nutrition Inc.	Rawhide Chew Sticks	15	$2.00

FONT

STYLE

SIZE

COLOR

MOVE THROUGH DATA

You can move through the data in a table to review and edit information.

If a table contains a lot of data, your computer screen may not be able to display all the data at once. You can scroll through records and fields to display data that does not appear on your screen.

MOVE THROUGH DATA

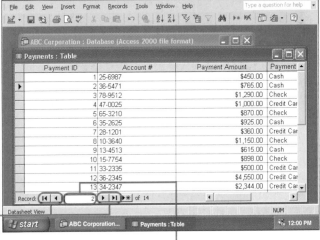

MOVE THROUGH RECORDS

1 Click any cell in the record you want to make the current record.

■ An arrow (▶) appears beside the current record.

■ This area displays the number of the current record and the total number of records in the table.

2 To move through the records, click one of the following buttons.

▮◀	First record
◀	Previous record
▶	Next record
▶▮	Last record

■ To quickly move to a specific record, double-click this area and then type the number of the record you want to display. Then press the **Enter** key.

How do I use my keyboard to move through data in a table?

Press on Keyboard	Description
Page Up	Move up one screen of records
Page Down	Move down one screen of records
Tab	Move to the next field in the current record
↑	Move up one record in the same field
↓	Move down one record in the same field

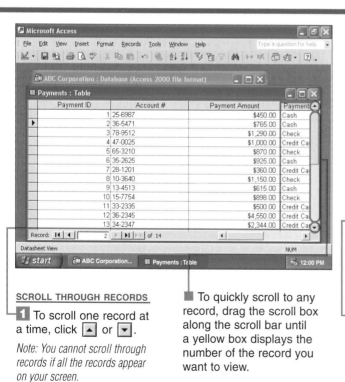

SCROLL THROUGH RECORDS

1 To scroll one record at a time, click ▲ or ▼.

Note: You cannot scroll through records if all the records appear on your screen.

■ To quickly scroll to any record, drag the scroll box along the scroll bar until a yellow box displays the number of the record you want to view.

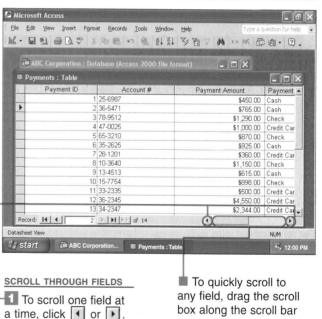

SCROLL THROUGH FIELDS

1 To scroll one field at a time, click ◄ or ►.

Note: You cannot scroll through fields if all the fields appear on your screen.

■ To quickly scroll to any field, drag the scroll box along the scroll bar until the field you want to view appears.

SELECT DATA

Before performing many tasks in a table, you must select the data you want to work with. Selected data appears highlighted on your screen.

SELECT DATA

SELECT A FIELD

1 Position the mouse I over the name of the field you want to select (I changes to ↓) and then click to select the field.

■ To select multiple fields, position the mouse I over the name of the first field (I changes to ↓). Then drag the mouse ↓ until you highlight all the fields you want to select.

SELECT A RECORD

1 Position the mouse I over the area to the left of the record you want to select (I changes to →) and then click to select the record.

■ To select multiple records, position the mouse I over the area to the left of the first record (I changes to →). Then drag the mouse → until you highlight all the records you want to select.

How do I select all the information in a table?

■ To select all the information in a table, click the blank area ( ) to the left of the field names.

How do I deselect data?

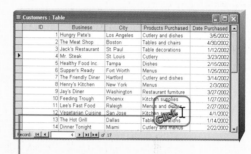

■ To deselect data, click anywhere in the table.

SELECT A CELL

1 Position the mouse I over the left edge of the cell you want to select (I changes to ✛) and then click to select the cell.

■ To select multiple cells, position the mouse I over the left edge of the first cell (I changes to ✛). Then drag the mouse ✛ until you highlight all the cells you want to select.

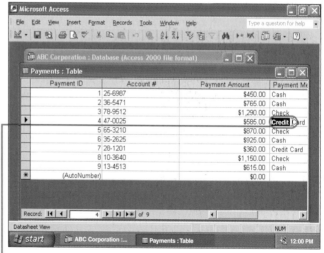

SELECT DATA IN A CELL

1 Position the mouse I over the left edge of the data and then drag the mouse I until you highlight all the data you want to select.

■ To quickly select a word, double-click the word.

EDIT DATA

You can edit the data in a table to correct a mistake or update the data.

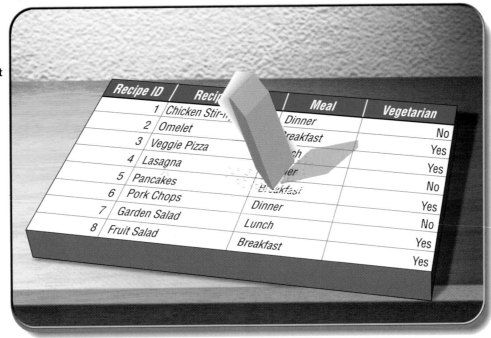

Access automatically saves the changes you make to the data in a table.

EDIT DATA

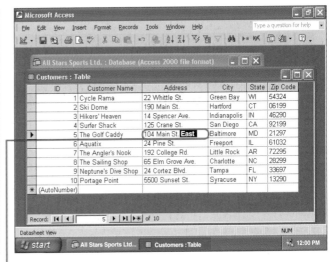

INSERT DATA

1 Click the location in the cell where you want to insert data.

■ A flashing insertion point appears in the cell, indicating where the data you type will appear.

Note: You can press the ← or → key to move the insertion point.

2 Type the data you want to insert.

DELETE DATA

1 Position the mouse I to the left of the data you want to delete.

2 Drag the mouse I until you highlight all the data you want to delete.

3 Press the Delete key to delete the data.

Note: To delete a single character, click to the right of the character you want to delete and then press the ◆Backspace key.

What are the symbols that appear to the left of the records in a table?

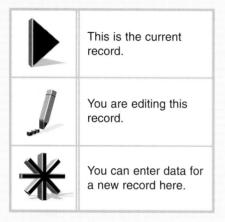

▶	This is the current record.
✏	You are editing this record.
✱	You can enter data for a new record here.

Why can't I edit the data in a cell?

You may be trying to edit data in a field that has the AutoNumber data type. A field that has the AutoNumber data type automatically numbers each record for you to uniquely identify each record. For more information on data types, see page 83.

REPLACE ALL DATA IN A CELL

1 Position the mouse I over the left edge of the cell containing the data you want to replace with new data (I changes to ⇨) and then click to select the cell.

■ The cell is highlighted.

2 Type the new data and then press the **Enter** key.

UNDO CHANGES

1 Click 🔄 to immediately undo your most recent change.

ZOOM INTO A CELL

You can zoom into any cell in a table to make the contents of the cell easier to review and edit.

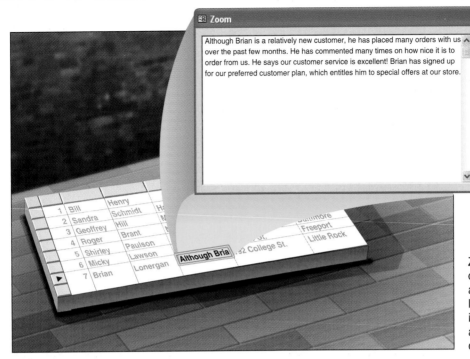

Zooming into a cell is useful when a cell contains a large amount of information, such as notes about a customer.

ZOOM INTO A CELL

1 Click the cell you want to zoom into.

2 Press and hold down the **Shift** key as you press the **F2** key.

■ The Zoom dialog box appears.

■ This area displays all the data in the cell. You can review and edit the data. To edit data, see page 56.

3 When you finish reviewing and editing the data, click **OK** to close the dialog box.

■ The table will display any changes you made to the data.

DISPLAY A SUBDATASHEET

When viewing the information in a table, you may be able to display a subdatasheet to view and edit related data from another table.

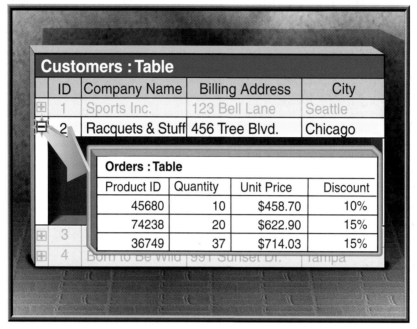

For example, when viewing a table containing customer information, you can display a subdatasheet to view the orders placed by a customer.

You can display a subdatasheet only when a table is related to another table. For information on relationships, see page 124.

DISPLAY A SUBDATASHEET

■ When information in a table relates to data in another table, a plus sign (🛨) appears beside each record.

1 To display related data from the other table, click the plus sign (🛨) beside a record (🛨 changes to ➖).

■ A subdatasheet appears, displaying the related data from the other table. You can review and edit the data. To edit data, see page 56.

2 To once again hide the subdatasheet, click the minus sign (➖) beside the record.

CHECK SPELLING

You can find and correct all the spelling errors in a table.

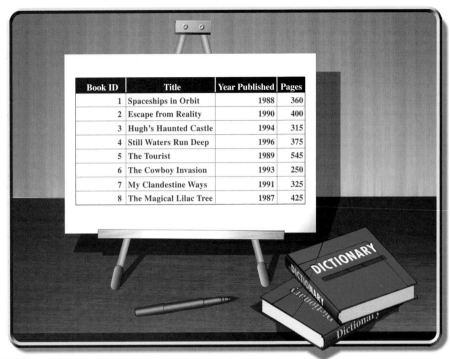

Book ID	Title	Year Published	Pages
1	Spaceships in Orbit	1988	360
2	Escape from Reality	1990	400
3	Hugh's Haunted Castle	1994	315
4	Still Waters Run Deep	1996	375
5	The Tourist	1989	545
6	The Cowboy Invasion	1993	250
7	My Clandestine Ways	1991	325
8	The Magical Lilac Tree	1987	425

Access compares every word in your table to words in its dictionary. If a word in your table does not exist in the dictionary, Access considers the word misspelled.

CHECK SPELLING

■1 To spell check your entire table, click any cell in the table.

Note: To spell check only part of your table, select the field, record or cell you want to check in the table. To select data in a table, see page 54.

■2 Click ✓ to start the spell check.

■ The Spelling dialog box appears if Access finds a misspelled word in your table.

■ This area displays the misspelled word.

■ This area displays suggestions for correcting the word.

Can Access automatically correct my typing mistakes?

Yes. Access automatically corrects common spelling errors as you type. Here are a few examples.

adn ⟶	and
alot ⟶	a lot
comittee ⟶	committee
don;t ⟶	don't
nwe ⟶	new
occurence ⟶	occurrence
recieve ⟶	receive
seperate ⟶	separate
teh ⟶	the

Will a spell check find all the errors in my table?

No. A spell check will find only spelling errors. Access will not find correctly spelled words used in the wrong context, such as "blew" in a Product Color field. You should carefully review your table to find this type of error.

Product Color	Qua
beige	
blew	
brown	
dark blue	
white	
yell...	

3 Click the suggestion you want to use to correct the word.

4 Click **Change** to correct the word in your table.

■ To skip the word and continue checking your table, click **Ignore**.

*Note: To skip the word and all other occurrences of the word in your table, click **Ignore All**.*

5 Correct or ignore misspelled words until this dialog box appears, telling you the spell check is complete.

6 Click **OK** to close the dialog box.

MOVE OR COPY DATA

You can move or copy data to a new location in your table.

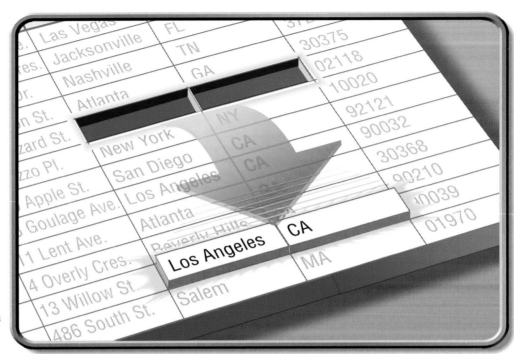

Moving data allows you to rearrange data in your table. When you move data, the data disappears from its original location.

Copying data allows you to repeat data in your table without having to retype the data. When you copy data, the data appears in both the original and new locations.

MOVE OR COPY DATA

1 To move or copy data in a cell, drag the mouse over the data until you highlight the data you want to move or copy.

■ To copy the entire contents of one or more cells, select the cell(s) containing the data you want to copy. To select cells, see page 54.

2 Click one of the following buttons.

✂ Move data

📋 Copy data

3 Click the location in the table where you want to place the data.

■ If you copied the entire contents of one or more cells, select the cell(s) where you want to place the data.

Why does the Clipboard task pane appear when I move or copy data?

When you move or copy data, the Clipboard task pane may appear. The Clipboard task pane displays the last items you have selected to move or copy. To place a clipboard item in your table, click the location where you want to place the item and then click the item in the task pane.

Note: To close the Clipboard task pane, click ⊠ *at the top of the task pane.*

4 Click 📋 to place the data in the new location.

■ The data appears in the new location.

COPY DATA DOWN ONE CELL

1 Click the cell directly below the data you want to copy.

2 Press and hold down the **Ctrl** key as you press the ' (apostrophe) key.

■ Access copies the data to the cell.

ADD A RECORD

You can add a new record to include additional information in your table. For example, you may want to add information about a new customer.

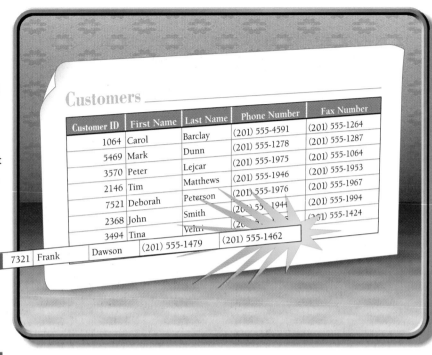

You can add a new record only to the end of your table. If you later want to change the order of the records in the table, you can sort the records. To sort records, see page 174.

ADD A RECORD

1 Click ▶* to add a new record to your table.

2 Click the first empty cell in the row.

3 Type the data that corresponds to the field and then press the Enter key to move to the next field.

■ In this example, the ID field automatically assigns a number to the new record.

4 Repeat step 3 until you finish entering all the data for the record.

■ Access automatically saves each new record you add to the table.

DELETE A RECORD

You can delete a record from a table to permanently remove information you no longer need. For example, you may want to remove information about a customer who no longer orders your products.

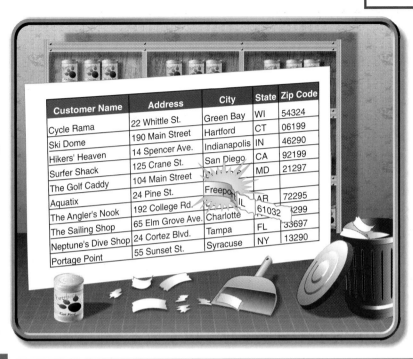

Deleting records saves storage space on your computer and keeps your database from becoming cluttered with unnecessary information.

When you delete a record, you may also want to delete any related records in other tables. For example, if you delete a company from your supplier table, you may also want to delete the company's products from your products table.

DELETE A RECORD

1 Position the mouse I over the area to the left of the record you want to delete (I changes to ➜) and then click to select the record.

2 Click 🔀 to delete the record.

■ The record disappears.

■ A warning dialog box appears.

3 Click **Yes** to permanently delete the record.

CHANGE THE FONT OF DATA

You can change the font, style, size and color of data in a table to customize the appearance of the table.

For example, you may want to use a smaller font size for your data to display more information on the screen at once.

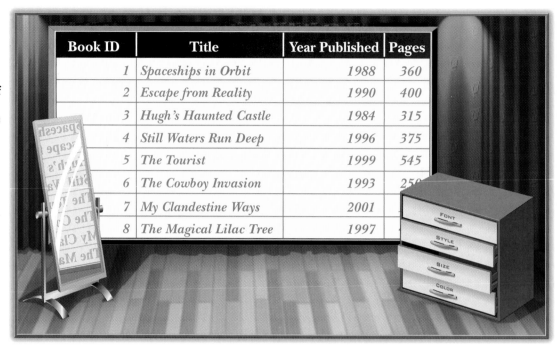

CHANGE THE FONT OF DATA

1 Click **Format**.

2 Click **Font**.

■ The Font dialog box appears.

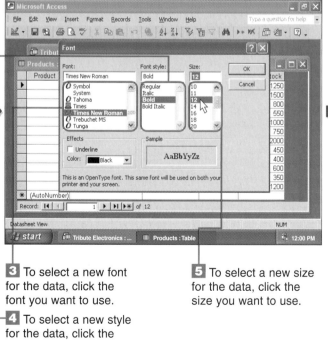

3 To select a new font for the data, click the font you want to use.

4 To select a new style for the data, click the style you want to use.

5 To select a new size for the data, click the size you want to use.

What determines which fonts are available on my computer?

The fonts available on your computer depend on the programs installed on your computer, the setup of your computer and the printer you are using.

What are the symbols that appear beside each font in the Font dialog box?

In the Font dialog box, a symbol appears beside each font to indicate the type of font. OpenType fonts (*O*) and TrueType fonts (**T**) will print exactly as they appear on your screen. Printer fonts ( ) may not print exactly as they appear on your screen.

6 To select a new color for the data, click this area to display a list of the available colors.

7 Click the color you want to use.

■ This area displays a preview of how the data will appear in your table.

8 Click **OK** to confirm your changes.

■ The data in your table displays the changes.

HIDE A FIELD

You can temporarily hide a field in a table to reduce the amount of information displayed on your screen.

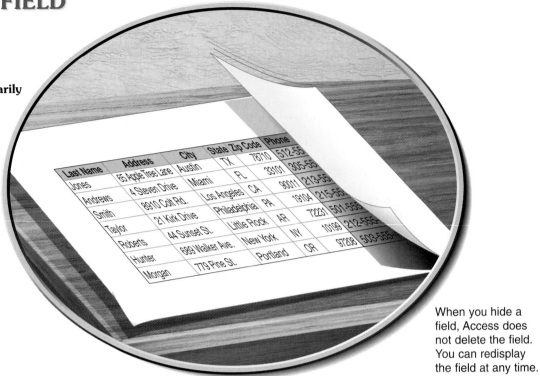

When you hide a field, Access does not delete the field. You can redisplay the field at any time.

HIDE A FIELD

1 Click the name of the field you want to hide. The field is highlighted.

Note: To hide more than one field at the same time, select the fields you want to hide. To select multiple fields, see page 54.

2 Click **Format**.

3 Click **Hide Columns**.

■ The field disappears from your table.

When would I hide a field?

Hiding a field can help you review information of interest in a table by removing unnecessary data from your screen. For example, if you want to browse through only the names and telephone numbers of your customers, you can hide the fields that display other information in your table.

First Name	Last Name	Phone No.	Add
Sue	Jones	(512) 555-8973	65
Matt	Andrews	(305) 555-9822	4 St
Jim	Smith	(213) 555-0231	8910
Karen	Taylor	(215) 555-4520	21 Kirk
Mandy	Roberts	(501) 555-8203	44 Sun

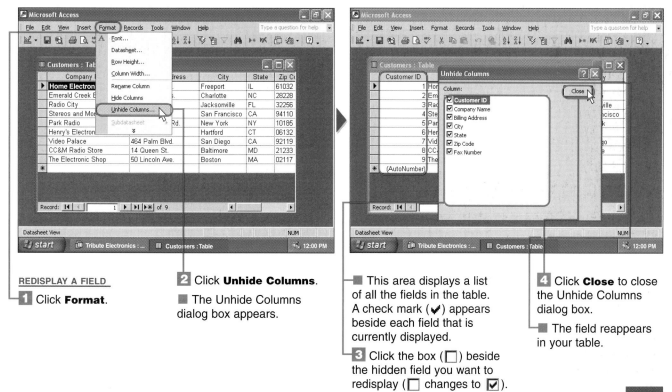

REDISPLAY A FIELD

1 Click **Format**.

2 Click **Unhide Columns**.

■ The Unhide Columns dialog box appears.

■ This area displays a list of all the fields in the table. A check mark (✔) appears beside each field that is currently displayed.

3 Click the box (☐) beside the hidden field you want to redisplay (☐ changes to ☑).

4 Click **Close** to close the Unhide Columns dialog box.

■ The field reappears in your table.

FREEZE A FIELD

You can freeze a field in a table so the field will remain on your screen at all times.

1 Click the name of the field you want to freeze. The field is highlighted.

Note: To freeze more than one field at the same time, select the fields you want to freeze. To select multiple fields, see page 54.

2 Click **Format**.

3 Click **Freeze Columns**.

Note: If Freeze Columns does not appear on the menu, position the mouse ▷ over the bottom of the menu to display all the menu options.

When would I freeze a field?

Freezing a field allows you to keep important data displayed on your screen as you move through data in a large table. For example, you can freeze a field that contains the product numbers in a table so the numbers will remain on your screen while you scroll through the product information.

4 Click any cell in the table to deselect the field.

■ Access moves the field to the left side of the table. The black vertical line to the right of the field indicates that the field is frozen.

■ The frozen field will remain on your screen as you move through the other fields in the table.

■ To move through the other fields in the table, click ◄ or ►.

UNFREEZE ALL FIELDS

1 Click **Format**.

2 Click **Unfreeze All Columns**.

Note: If Unfreeze All Columns does not appear on the menu, position the mouse ⌖ over the bottom of the menu to display all the menu options.

■ When you unfreeze a field, Access will not return the field to its original location in the table. To rearrange fields in a table, see page 43.

Design Tables

Would you like to customize your tables to better suit your needs? In this chapter, you will learn how to add and delete fields, create a lookup column and much more.

CHANGE THE VIEW OF A TABLE

You can view a table in four different ways. Each view allows you to perform different tasks.

CHANGE THE VIEW OF A TABLE

■ In this example, the table appears in the Datasheet view.

1 Click ⋅ in this area to display the table in a different view.

2 Click the view you want to use.

■ The table appears in the view you selected.

■ In this example, the View button changed from ⬚ to ⬚ .

■ To quickly switch between the Datasheet (⬚) and Design (⬚) views, click the View button.

THE TABLE VIEWS

Design View

The Design view displays the structure of a table. You can change the settings in this view to specify the kind of information you can enter into a table.

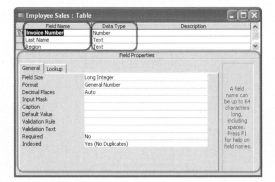

The **Field Name** area displays the name of each field in a table.

The **Data Type** area displays the type of data you can enter into each field, such as text or numbers.

The **Field Properties** area shows the properties for the current field.

Datasheet View

The Datasheet view displays all the records in a table. The field names appear across the top of the window and the information for one record appears in each row. You can review, enter and edit records in this view.

Invoice Number	Last Name	Region	Period	Sales
23452	Grey	North	Quarter 1	$15,000.00
23453	Lampley	South	Quarter 3	$12,400.00
23454	Spears	Central	Quarter 2	$19,000.00
23455	Grey	North	Quarter 2	$22,900.00
23456	Lampley	South	Quarter 1	$28,900.00
23457	Spears	Central	Quarter 3	$18,000.00
23458	Grey	North	Quarter 3	$21,000.00
23459	Lampley	South	Quarter 2	$19,500.00
23460	Spears	Central	Quarter 1	$29,000.00
23461	Harris	Central	Quarter 1	$16,000.00
23462	Oberbroeckling	North	Quarter 1	$16,800.00
23463	Martin	South	Quarter 3	$18,200.00
23464	Oberbroeckling	North	Quarter 2	$23,000.00

Record: 1 of 18

PivotTable View

The PivotTable view allows you to summarize and analyze the data in a table. When you first display a table in this view, the PivotTable is empty and you must add the fields you want the PivotTable to display. For information on using the PivotTable view, see page 232.

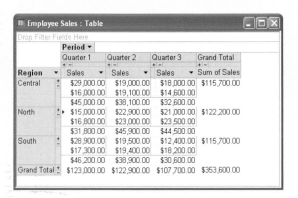

PivotChart View

The PivotChart view allows you to display a graphical summary of the data in a table. When you first display a table in this view, the PivotChart is empty and you must add the fields you want the PivotChart to display. For information on using the PivotChart view, see page 238.

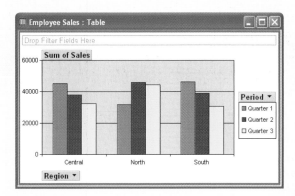

ADD A FIELD

You can add a field to a table when you want the table to include an additional category of information.

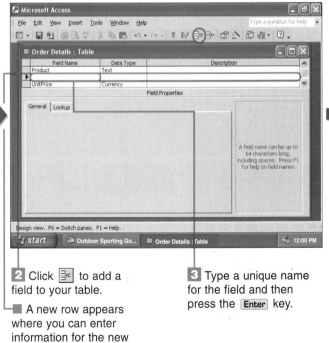

A field is a specific category of information in a table, such as the phone numbers of all your clients.

1 Click the name of the field you want to appear after the new field. A triangle (▶) appears beside the field name.

■ To add a field to the end of your table, click the area directly below the last field name. Then skip to step **3**.

2 Click 🔻 to add a field to your table.

■ A new row appears where you can enter information for the new field.

3 Type a unique name for the field and then press the **Enter** key.

76

What should I consider when adding fields to a table?

Make sure each field you add to a table relates directly to the subject of the table. You should also make sure you separate the information you want to include in a table into its smallest parts, such as First Name and Last Name.

What data type should I select for my new field?

The data type you should select depends on the type of information you want to enter in the field. For example, you can choose the Currency data type for a field you want to contain monetary values, such as the prices of products. For more information on data types, see page 82.

■ Access automatically sets the data type for the new field to **Text**.

4 To specify a different data type for the new field, click the arrow (🔽) to display a list of data types.

5 Click the appropriate data type for the field.

6 Click 🖫 to save your change.

7 Click 🔲 to display your table in the Datasheet view.

■ The new field appears in your table.

■ To return to the Design view, click 🖾.

DELETE A FIELD

If you no longer need a field, you can permanently delete the field from a table.

Before you delete a field, make sure the field is not used in any other objects in your database, such as a form, query or report.

You cannot delete a field used to create a relationship with another table in your database. For information on relationships, see page 124.

DELETE A FIELD

1 Click the name of the field you want to delete.

2 Click ⊟⁺ to delete the field.

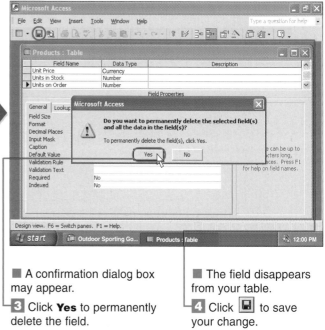

■ A confirmation dialog box may appear.

3 Click **Yes** to permanently delete the field.

■ The field disappears from your table.

4 Click 🖫 to save your change.

You can change
the order of
fields to better
organize the
information
in a table.

When you rearrange
fields in the Design
view, Access also
displays the changes
in the Datasheet
view of a table. For
information on the
views of a table, see
page 74.

REARRANGE FIELDS

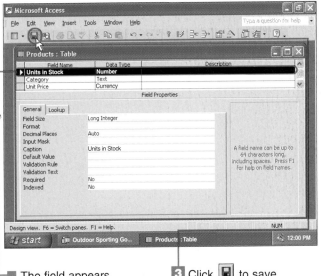

1 Click the area to the
left of the field you want
to move. The field is
highlighted.

2 Position the mouse I
over the area to the left of
the field (I changes to ⇩)
and then drag the field to
a new location.

■ A thick line shows
where the field will appear.

■ The field appears
in the new location.

3 Click 🖫 to save
your change.

DISPLAY FIELD PROPERTIES

You can display the properties for each field in a table. The field properties are a set of characteristics that control how data is entered, displayed and stored in a field.

For example, a field property can specify the maximum number of characters a field can accept.

DISPLAY FIELD PROPERTIES

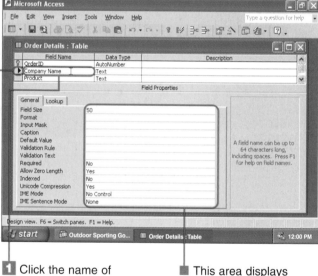

■ This area displays the field name and data type for each field in your table.

■ You can click ⏶ or ⏷ to browse through the fields.

1 Click the name of a field to display the properties for the field.

■ A triangle (▶) appears beside the field name.

■ This area displays the properties for the field you selected.

Note: The available properties depend on the data type of the field. For information on data types, see page 83.

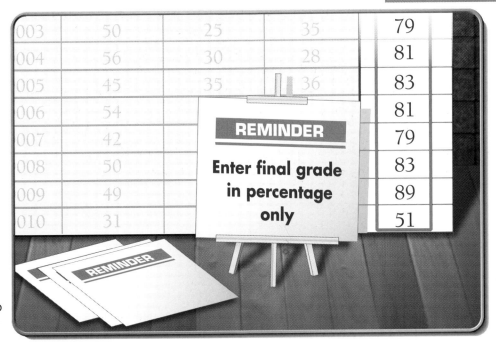

You can add a
description to
a field to help
you determine
the kind of
information
you should
enter in the
field.

REMINDER

**Enter final grade
in percentage
only**

You can use up to
255 characters to
describe a field.

ADD A FIELD DESCRIPTION

1 Click the Description
area for the field you want
to add a description to.

2 Type the description.

3 Click 🔲 to save
your change.

4 Click 🔳 to
display your table in
the Datasheet view.

5 Click anywhere in
the field you added the
description to.

■ The description for the
field appears in this area.

■ To return to the Design
view, click 🔳.

CHANGE A DATA TYPE

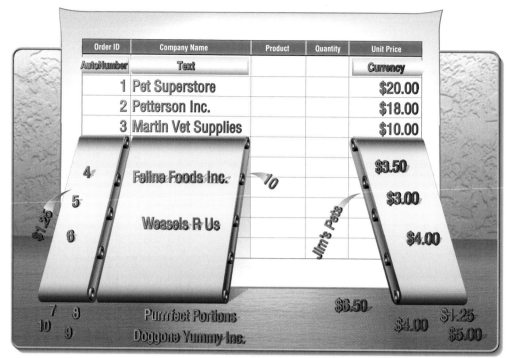

Order ID	Company Name	Product	Quantity	Unit Price
AutoNumber	Text			Currency
1	Pet Superstore			$20.00
2	Petterson Inc.			$18.00
3	Martin Vet Supplies			$10.00

You can change the type of data you can enter into a field.

Changing the data type for a field helps prevent errors when entering data in the field. Access will not accept data that does not match the data type you specify. For example, you cannot enter text into a field with the Number data type.

CHANGE A DATA TYPE

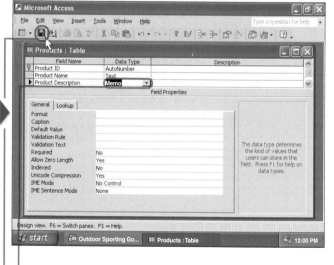

1 Click the Data Type area for the field you want to change to a new data type. An arrow (▼) appears.

2 Click the arrow (▼) to display a list of data types.

3 Click the data type you want the field to use.

■ The field changes to the new data type.

4 Click ⊞ to save your change.

■ If you change the data type for a field that contains data, Access will display an error message if it encounters errors while converting the data. To delete the data that is causing the errors, click **Yes**. To cancel the change, click **No**.

DATA TYPES

Text

Accepts entries up to 255 characters long that include any combination of text and numbers, such as names or addresses. Make sure you use this data type for numbers you will not use in calculations, such as phone numbers, product numbers or zip codes.

Memo

Accepts entries up to 65,536 characters long that include any combination of text and numbers, such as notes, comments or descriptions.

Number

Accepts numbers you want to use in calculations. For calculations that involve monetary values, use the Currency data type.

Date/Time

Accepts only dates and times.

Currency

Accepts monetary values.

AutoNumber

Automatically numbers each record for you.

Yes/No

Accepts only one of two values—Yes/No, True/False or On/Off.

OLE Object

Accepts OLE objects. An OLE object is an item created in another program, such as a document, spreadsheet, picture or sound.

Hyperlink

Accepts hyperlinks you can select to jump to a document or Web page.

SELECT A FORMAT

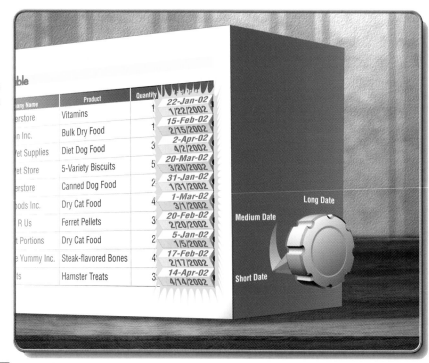

You can select a format to customize the way information appears in a field. For example, you can select the way you want numbers or dates to appear.

Selecting a format will not change how information is stored in a table.

SELECT A FORMAT

1 Click the field that contains the data you want to display in a new format.

2 Click the area beside **Format**. An arrow (▾) appears.

3 Click the arrow (▾) to display a list of formats.

Note: A list of formats only appears for fields with the Number, Date/Time, Currency, AutoNumber or Yes/No data type. For information on data types, see page 82.

4 Click the format you want to use.

What formats are available?

Number, Currency and AutoNumber Formats	
General Number	3456.789
Currency	$3,456.79
Euro	€3,456.79
Fixed	3456.79
Standard	3,456.79
Percent	123.00%
Scientific	3.46E+03

Date/Time Formats	
General Date	6/19/2002 5:34:23 PM
Long Date	Wednesday, June 19, 2002
Medium Date	19-Jun-02
Short Date	6/19/2002
Long Time	5:34:23 PM
Medium Time	5:34 PM
Short Time	17:34

■ The format you selected appears in this area.

5 Click 🖫 to save your change.

6 Click 🧾 to display your table in the Datasheet view.

■ The data displays the format you selected.

■ Access will automatically change any data you enter in the field to the new format. For example, Access will automatically change 1234 to $1,234.00.

■ To return to the Design view, click 🔣.

CHANGE THE FIELD SIZE

You can change the size of a text or number field to specify the maximum size of data that you can enter in the field.

First Name	Last Name	City
Jim	Schmith	New York
Brenda	Petterson	Boston
Jim	Martin	San Diego
Melanie	Robinson	Jacksonville
Susan	Hughes	Nashville
Allen	Toppins	Atlanta

State

N Y
M A
C A
F L
T N
G A

You should select the smallest possible field size for data. Smaller field sizes can be processed faster, require less memory and use less storage space.

Changing the field size also helps you reduce errors when entering data. For example, if you set the size of a text field to 2, you can enter CA but not California.

TEXT FIELDS

1 Click the field you want to accept a maximum number of characters.

■ The area beside Field Size displays the maximum number of characters you can currently type in the field. The default setting is 50.

2 Double-click the number to highlight the number.

3 Type the maximum number of characters you want the field to accept.

Note: You can enter a number from 0 to 255.

4 Click 🖫 to save your change.

■ A warning dialog box appears if you are reducing the size of a text field that contains data. Access will shorten any data that is longer than the new field size. To continue, click **Yes**.

What field sizes are available for number fields?

Access offers several field sizes for number fields. Some field sizes allow you to only enter whole numbers. If you want to be able to enter numbers with decimal places, such as 1.23, you must select the Single, Double or Decimal field size.

Field Size	Range	Decimal Places
Byte	0 to 255	none
Integer	-32,768 to 32,767	none
Long Integer	-2.1×10^9 to 2.1×10^9	none
Single	-3.4×10^{38} to 3.4×10^{38}	7
Double	-1.8×10^{308} to 1.8×10^{308}	15
Decimal	-10^{28} to 10^{28}	28

NUMBER FIELDS

1 Click the field you want to only accept a certain type of number.

2 Click the area beside **Field Size**. An arrow (⏷) appears.

3 Click the arrow (⏷) to display a list of options.

4 Click the type of number you want the field to accept.

5 Click 🖫 to save your change.

■ A warning dialog box appears if you are reducing the size of a number field that contains data. Access will change or delete data that is larger than the new field size. To continue, click **Yes**.

CHANGE THE NUMBER OF DECIMAL PLACES

You can specify
how many decimal
places you want
numbers to
display in a field.

You can
display up to
15 decimal
places after
the decimal
point.

CHANGE THE NUMBER OF DECIMAL PLACES

1 Click the field that
contains the data you
want to display a specific
number of decimal places.

2 Click the area beside
Decimal Places. An
arrow (▼) appears.

3 Click the arrow (▼)
to display a list of decimal
place options.

4 Click the number
of decimal places you
want the data in the
field to display.

*Note: The Auto option will
usually display numbers
with two decimal places.*

Will changing the number of decimal places affect the way numbers are stored?

Changing the number of decimal places will not affect the way numbers are stored or used in calculations. For example, if you change the number of decimal places to 1, the number 2.3456 will be displayed as 2.3, but Access will store and perform calculations using the number 2.3456.

Why doesn't my data display the number of decimal places I specified?

Changing the number of decimal places will not change the appearance of numbers if the Format property of the field is blank or set to General Number. To change the Format property of a field, see page 84.

■ The number of decimal places you selected appears in this area.

5 Click 🖫 to save your change.

6 Click 🖩 to display your table in the Datasheet view.

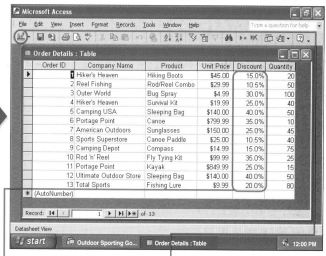

■ The data displays the number of decimal places you specified.

■ When you enter data in the field, Access will automatically display the data with the correct number of decimal places.

Note: If Access changes decimal places you type to zeros (example: 12.34 changes to 12.00), you need to change the field size. To change the field size, see page 86.

■ To return to the Design view, click 🖉.

ADD A CAPTION

You can add a caption to a field. The caption will appear as the heading for the field instead of the field name.

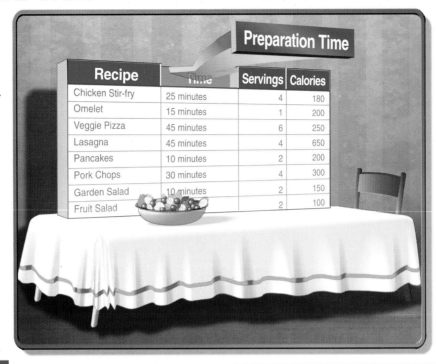

A caption can be longer and more descriptive than a field name.

After you add a caption to a field, any forms, reports or queries you create that include the field will display the caption instead of the field name.

ADD A CAPTION

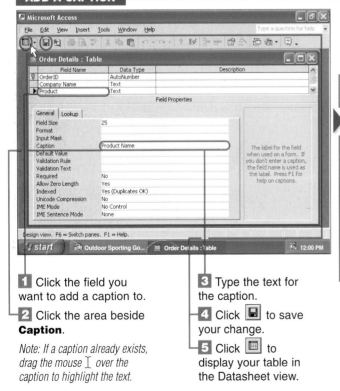

1 Click the field you want to add a caption to.

2 Click the area beside **Caption**.

Note: If a caption already exists, drag the mouse I over the caption to highlight the text.

3 Type the text for the caption.

4 Click 🖫 to save your change.

5 Click 🖷 to display your table in the Datasheet view.

■ The caption you entered replaces the field name in your table.

■ To return to the Design view, click 🖳.

You can specify
a value that you
want to appear
automatically in a
field each time you
add a new record.
Setting a default
value saves you
from having to
repeatedly type
the same data.

Company	Address	City	State	Phone
	258 Linton Ave.	San Diego	**CA**	(619) 555-1694
	50 Tree Lane	Los Angeles	**CA**	(213) 555-1507
	68 Cracker Ave.	San Diego	**CA**	(619) 555-246
Company	26 Arnold Cres.	Los Angeles	**CA**	(213) 555-3579
	47 Crosby Ave.	Los Angeles	**CA**	(213) 555-4 04
Company	401 Idon Dr.	San Francisco	**CA**	(415) 555-5104
Products	10 Heldon St.	San Francisco	**CA**	(415) 555-9
Shade Inc.	36 Buzzard St.	Los Angeles	**CA**	(21

For example,
if most of your
customers live in
California, you can
set "California" as
the default value
for the State field.

In a field that
contains dates,
such as an Order
Date field, you
can set the current
date as the default
value for the field.

SET A DEFAULT VALUE

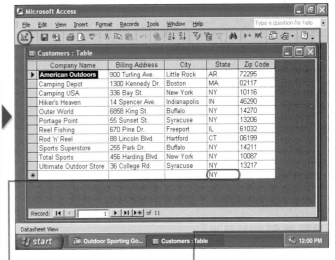

1 Click the field you want
to have a default value.

2 Click the area beside
Default Value.

3 Type the text or
number you want to
set as the default value.

*Note: To set the current date as
the default value, type* ***=Date()****.*

4 Click 🖫 to save
your change.

5 Click 🖳 to display
your table in the
Datasheet view.

■ The default value
automatically appears
in the field each time
you add a new record.
You can accept the
default value or type
another value.

*Note: Setting a default value
will not affect existing data
in the field.*

■ To return to the
Design view, click 🖳.

DATA ENTRY REQUIRED

You can specify that a field must contain data for each record. This prevents you from leaving out important information when entering data.

For example, a table containing invoice information can require data in the Invoice Number field.

Item	Qty	Amount	Invoice #
Tennis Balls	505	$3.00	16437
Golf Clubs	736	$550.95	16438
Biking Shorts	377	$34.99	16439
Running Shoes	638	$99.49	16440
Hats	894	$15.99	16441

DATA REQUIRED

DATA ENTRY REQUIRED

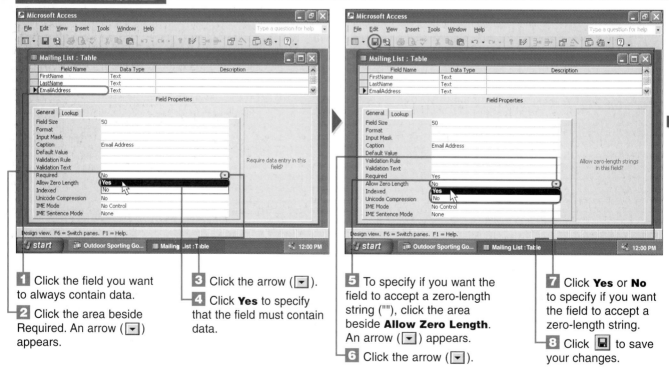

1 Click the field you want to always contain data.

2 Click the area beside Required. An arrow (▾) appears.

3 Click the arrow (▾).

4 Click **Yes** to specify that the field must contain data.

5 To specify if you want the field to accept a zero-length string (""), click the area beside **Allow Zero Length**. An arrow (▾) appears.

6 Click the arrow (▾).

7 Click **Yes** or **No** to specify if you want the field to accept a zero-length string.

8 Click 🖫 to save your changes.

What is a zero-length string?

A zero-length string ("") indicates that no data exists for the field. A zero-length string is useful when a field is set to require data, but no data exists. For example, if the Fax number field must contain data, but a customer does not have a fax number, you can enter a zero-length string in the field. You can allow zero-length strings only in fields with the Text, Memo or Hyperlink data type. For information on data types, see page 82.

To enter a zero-length string, type "" in a cell. When you enter a zero-length string, the cell will appear empty.

ID	First Name	Last Name	Phone	Fax
1	Theresa	Garcia	555-4433	555-4434
2	Daniel	Goodland	555-1234	
3	Susan	Hughes	555-6677	555-6678
4	Greg	Kilkenny	555-1215	555-1216
5	Stephen	MacDonald	555-2200	
6	Jim	Smith	555-1543	555-1550
7	Allen	Toppins	555-6235	555-6236
8	Linda	Vieira	555-8976	

CAN CONTAIN
ZERO-LENGTH
STRINGS

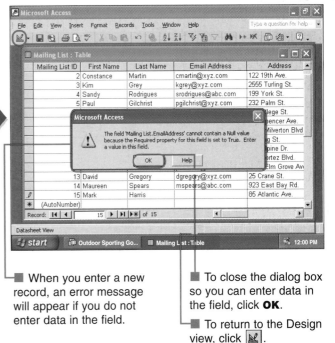

■ If your table contains data, a dialog box appears, asking if you want to check if the field contains data for all existing records.

9 If you do not want to check the field, click **No**.

*Note: If you want to check the field, click **Yes**.*

10 Click [image] to display your table in the Datasheet view.

■ When you enter a new record, an error message will appear if you do not enter data in the field.

■ To close the dialog box so you can enter data in the field, click **OK**.

■ To return to the Design view, click [image].

ADD A VALIDATION RULE

You can add a validation rule to help reduce errors when entering data in a field. A field that uses a validation rule can only accept data that meets the requirements you specify.

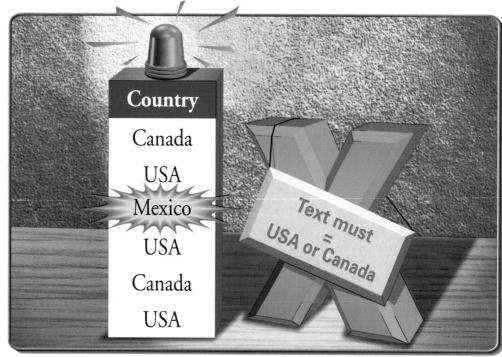

ADD A VALIDATION RULE

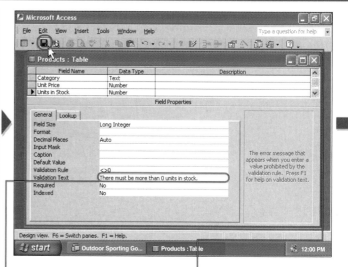

1 Click the field you want to use a validation rule.

2 Click the area beside **Validation Rule**.

3 Type the validation rule you want to use to limit the data you can enter into the field.

Note: For examples of validation rules, see the top of page 95.

4 To create the error message you want to appear when you enter incorrect data, click the area beside **Validation Text**.

5 Type the error message you want to appear.

Note: If you do not specify an error message, Access will display a standard message.

6 Click 🔲 to save your changes.

What validation rules can I use?

Here are some examples of validation rules that you can use. For more examples, see page 212.

RULE	DESCRIPTION
<1000	Must be less than 1000
<>0	Cannot be zero
Between 100 and 200	Must be between 100 and 200
USA or Canada	Must be USA or Canada
Like "????"	Must have 4 characters
Like "##"	Must have 2 numbers

VALIDATION RULES

What should my error message contain?

When you enter incorrect data, the error message that appears should clearly explain why the data you entered is incorrect. For example, the error message "You must enter a number between 1 and 100" is more informative than the message "Data Rejected."

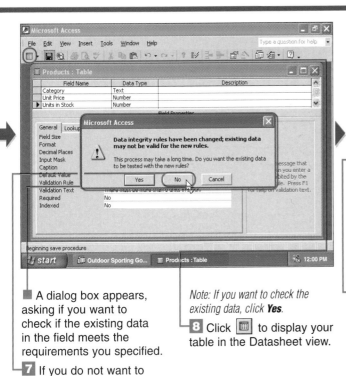

■ A dialog box appears, asking if you want to check if the existing data in the field meets the requirements you specified.

7 If you do not want to check the existing data, click **No**.

Note: If you want to check the existing data, click Yes.

8 Click 🔳 to display your table in the Datasheet view.

■ When you enter data that does not meet the requirements you specified for the field, the error message you typed in step **5** will appear.

■ To close the dialog box so you can enter different data, click **OK**.

■ To return to the Design view, click 🔳.

CREATE AN INPUT MASK

You can create an input mask to control the type of information you can enter in a field. Input masks reduce errors and ensure data has a consistent appearance.

The Input Mask Wizard provides commonly used input masks that you can choose from.

You can use the Input Mask Wizard only in fields with the Text or Date/Time data type. For information on data types, see page 82.

Input Mask	Data Appearance
Phone Number	(2 0 6) 5 5 5 – 1 2 1 2
Social Security Number	5 3 1 – 8 6 – 7 1 8 0
Zip Code	9 8 0 5 2 – 6 3 9 9
Extension	6 3 2 1 5
Password	* * * * * * *
Long Time	3 : 1 2 : 0 0 A M
Short Date	9 / 2 7 / 1 9 6 9
Short Time	0 3 : 1 2
Medium Time	0 3 : 1 2 A M
Medium Date	2 7 – S e p – 6 9

CREATE AN INPUT MASK USING THE WIZARD

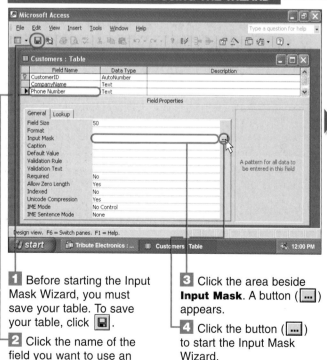

1 Before starting the Input Mask Wizard, you must save your table. To save your table, click 💾.

2 Click the name of the field you want to use an input mask.

3 Click the area beside **Input Mask**. A button (⋯) appears.

4 Click the button (⋯) to start the Input Mask Wizard.

■ The Input Mask Wizard appears.

■ This area displays the available input masks and how the data will appear in the field.

5 Click the input mask you want to use.

6 To try the input mask you selected, press the Tab key and then type the appropriate data.

7 Click **Next** to continue.

Why does a dialog box appear when I try to start the Input Mask Wizard?

When you try to start the Input Mask Wizard for the first time, a dialog box appears, stating that the wizard is not installed on your computer. To install the wizard, insert the CD you used to install Access into your CD drive and then click **Yes** to install the wizard.

How can an input mask save me time when I enter data in a field?

Input masks can save you time by automatically entering characters for you, such as brackets ( ), hyphens (-) and slashes (/). For example, when you type **2015551234** in a field that uses the Phone Number input mask, Access will change the data to **(201) 555-1234**.

■ This area displays the input mask you selected.

8 To select a placeholder character for the input mask, click ▼ in this area.

9 Click the placeholder character you want to use.

Note: When you enter data in the field, the data you type will replace the placeholder characters. For example, (___) ___-____ will change to (555) 555-3874.

10 To try the input mask with the placeholder character you selected, press the `Tab` key and then type the appropriate data.

11 Click **Next** to continue.

■ You can click **Back** at any time to return to a previous step and change your selections.

CONTINUED ▶

CREATE AN INPUT MASK

When you create an input mask, the wizard may ask how you want to store the data you enter in the field.

You can store data with or without symbols. Storing data without symbols saves storage space on your computer.

CREATE AN INPUT MASK USING THE WIZARD (CONTINUED)

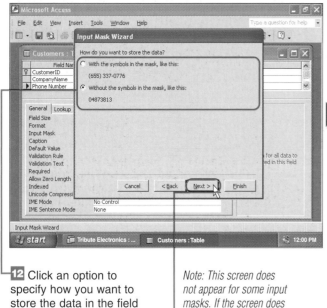

12 Click an option to specify how you want to store the data in the field (○ changes to ⊙).

Note: This screen does not appear for some input masks. If the screen does not appear, skip to step 14.

13 Click **Next** to continue.

■ This message appears when you have provided all the information the wizard needs to create the input mask.

14 Click **Finish** to close the wizard.

After creating an input mask, why doesn't the data I enter appear the way I expect?

After you use an input mask to enter data in a field, Access will display the data using the format set for the field. The format determines how data will appear in a field. For example, if you enter the date **09/15/2002** in a field that uses the Short Date input mask and the Long Date format, the date will automatically change to **Sunday, September 15, 2002** after you press the Enter key. To select a format for a field, see page 84.

■ This area displays the input mask.

15 Click 🔲 to save the input mask.

16 Click 🔳 to display your table in the Datasheet view.

USE AN INPUT MASK

1 Click an empty cell in the field that uses the input mask.

2 To move to the beginning of the cell, press the Home key.

3 Type the appropriate data.

Note: Access will only accept characters specified by the input mask. For example, you can only enter numbers in a field that uses the Phone Number input mask.

CONTINUED

CREATE AN INPUT MASK

You can create your own input mask to establish a pattern for data you can enter in a field.

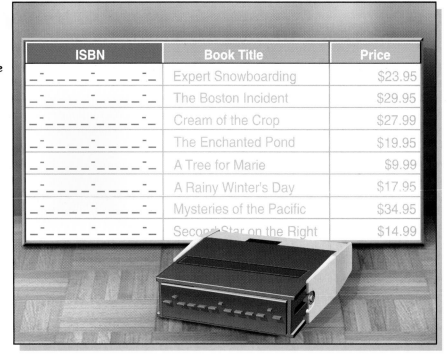

You may want to create your own input mask if the Input Mask Wizard does not offer an input mask that suits the data you want to enter in a field. To create an input mask using the wizard, see page 96.

CREATE YOUR OWN INPUT MASK

1 Click the name of the field you want to use an input mask.

2 Click the area beside **Input Mask**.

3 Type the input mask you want to use.

4 Click 🖫 to save your change.

5 Click 🖼 to display your table in the Datasheet view.

How do I remove an input mask?

If you no longer want a field to use an input mask, you can delete the input mask. In the Input Mask area for the field, position the mouse I to the left of the input mask and then drag the mouse I until you highlight the entire input mask. Then press the Delete key to delete the input mask.

Format
Input Mask   !\(999") "000\-0000;;_
Caption
Default Value
Validation Rule

How can creating my own input mask save me time when entering data?

Input masks can save you time by automatically entering characters for you. For example, if your invoice numbers always begin with **INV**, you can create an input mask that will automatically enter these characters for you.

Invoice ID	Company	Product
INV ____	Ski World	Ski goggles
INV ____	Big League Inc.	T-ball stand
INV ____	Varsity Supply	Lacrosse stick
INV ____	Ski World	Snowboard

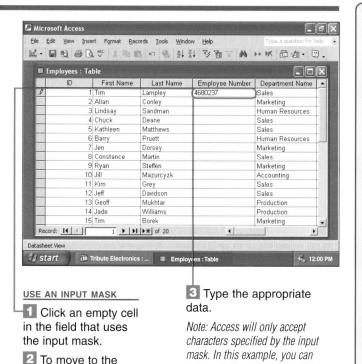

USE AN INPUT MASK

1 Click an empty cell in the field that uses the input mask.

2 To move to the beginning of the cell, press the Home key.

3 Type the appropriate data.

Note: Access will only accept characters specified by the input mask. In this example, you can enter only 7 numbers in the field.

INPUT MASK CHARACTERS

You can use these characters to create an input mask.

0
Numbers 0 to 9, required. Plus (+) and minus (-) signs not allowed.

9
Number or space, optional. Plus (+) and minus (-) signs not allowed.

#
Number or space, optional. Plus (+) and minus (-) signs allowed.

L
Letters A to Z, required.

?
Letters A to Z, optional.

A
Letter or number, required.

a
Letter or number, optional.

&
Character or space, required.

C
Character or space, optional.

. , : ; - /
Decimal point and thousands, date and time separators.

<
Convert the following characters to lowercase.

>
Convert the following characters to uppercase.

!
Display characters from right to left, rather than from left to right.

****
Display the following input mask character. For example, \& will display &.

Password
Display an asterisk (*) for each character you type.

CREATE A FIELD TO STORE PICTURES

You can create a field that allows you to add a picture to each record in a table.

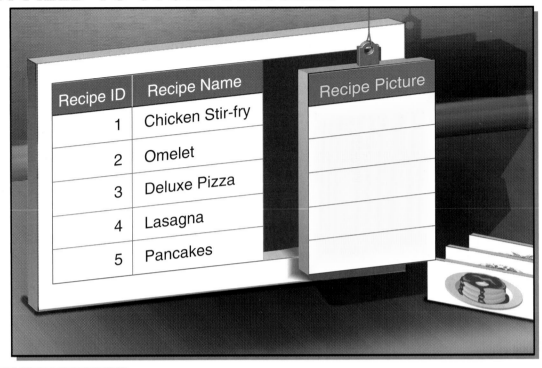

For example, you can create a field to store pictures of employees, houses for sale, artwork, recipes or products.

CREATE A FIELD TO STORE PICTURES

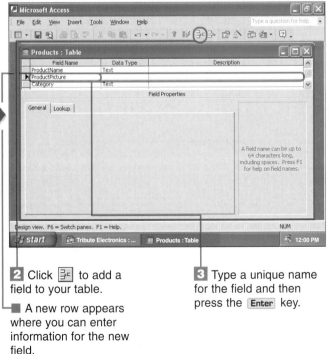

1 To create a field that will store pictures, click the name of the field you want to appear after the new field. A triangle (▶) appears beside the field name.

■ To add a field that will store pictures to the end of your table, click the area directly below the last field name. Then skip to step **3**.

2 Click 🔤 to add a field to your table.

■ A new row appears where you can enter information for the new field.

3 Type a unique name for the field and then press the Enter key.

Will the pictures I add to my table appear on a form?

When you create a form using a table that includes pictures, the form will display the pictures.

Can I add other types of files to a table?

You can add files such as documents, spreadsheets, sounds and videos to a table as you would add pictures to a table. When you double-click the cell containing a file in a table, the appropriate program will open and display or play the file.

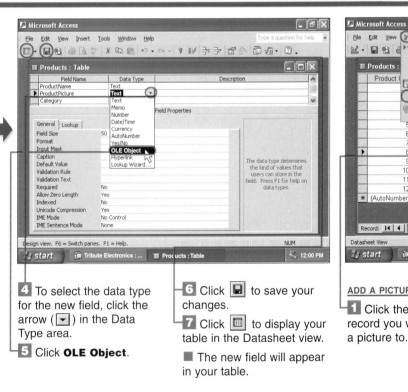

-4 To select the data type for the new field, click the arrow (▼) in the Data Type area.

-5 Click **OLE Object**.

-6 Click 🖫 to save your changes.

-7 Click 🔲 to display your table in the Datasheet view.

■ The new field will appear in your table.

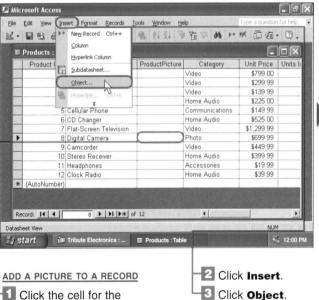

ADD A PICTURE TO A RECORD

-1 Click the cell for the record you want to add a picture to.

-2 Click **Insert**.

-3 Click **Object**.

CONTINUED ▶

CREATE A FIELD TO STORE PICTURES

When adding a picture to a record in a table, you must specify where the picture is stored on your computer.

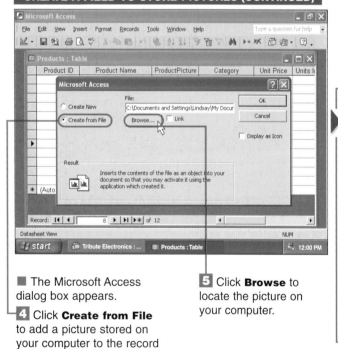

■ The Microsoft Access dialog box appears.

4 Click **Create from File** to add a picture stored on your computer to the record (○ changes to ⊙).

5 Click **Browse** to locate the picture on your computer.

■ This area shows the location of the displayed files. You can click this area to change the location.

6 Click the name of the picture you want to add to the record.

7 Click **OK** to confirm your selection.

Why would I add a link to a picture to my table?

When you add a link to a picture, Access creates a connection to the original picture on your computer. Changes you make to the original picture will affect the picture in the table. If you choose not to add a link to a picture, Access stores a copy of the picture in your database. Changes you make to the original picture will not affect the picture in the table.

How do I remove a picture I added to my table?

To remove a picture from a table, click the cell containing the picture and then press the Delete key. Access will not delete the original picture stored on your computer.

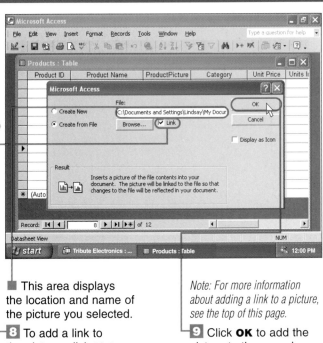

■ This area displays the location and name of the picture you selected.

8 To add a link to the picture, click **Link** (☐ changes to ☑).

Note: For more information about adding a link to a picture, see the top of this page.

9 Click **OK** to add the picture to the record.

■ The cell displays information about the picture you added to the record.

■ To add pictures to other records, repeat steps 1 to 9 starting on page 103 for each record.

VIEW A PICTURE

1 To view a picture, double-click the cell containing the picture you want to view.

CREATE A LOOKUP COLUMN

You can create a lookup column, which displays a list of values that you can choose from when entering information in a field.

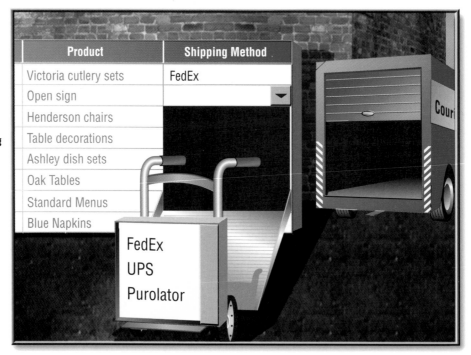

CREATE A LOOKUP COLUMN

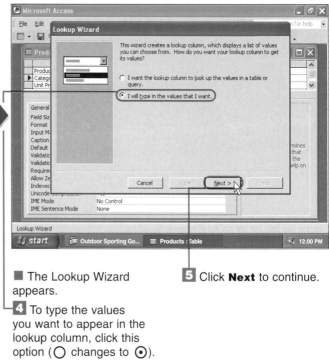

1 Click the Data Type area for the field you want to use a lookup column. An arrow (▼) appears.

2 Click the arrow (▼) to display a list of data types.

3 Click **Lookup Wizard**.

■ The Lookup Wizard appears.

4 To type the values you want to appear in the lookup column, click this option (○ changes to ⊙).

5 Click **Next** to continue.

106

Why would I create a lookup column?

Creating a lookup column is useful if you repeatedly enter the same values in a field. For example, if your customers reside in three states, you can create a lookup column that displays the three states, such as CA, TX and IL.

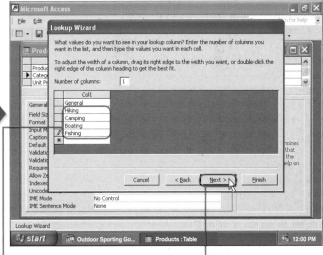

◀ **6** Click this area and then type the first value you want to appear in the lookup column.

■ To adjust the width of the lookup column, position the mouse ⬚ over the right edge of the column heading (⬚ changes to ↔) and then drag the column edge to the width you want.

7 To enter the next value, press the Tab key and then type the value.

8 Repeat step 7 for each value you want to appear in the lookup column.

9 When you finish entering all the values for the lookup column, click **Next** to continue.

CONTINUED ▶

CREATE A LOOKUP COLUMN

When entering data in a field, you can select a value from a lookup column to save time.

Selecting a value from a lookup column can also prevent errors such as typing mistakes and ensure that you enter the correct type of data in a field.

CREATE A LOOKUP COLUMN (CONTINUED)

10 This area displays the name of the field that will offer the lookup column. To change the field name, type a new name.

11 Click **Finish** to create the lookup column.

12 Click 🖫 to save your changes.

13 To display your table in the Datasheet view, click 🖩 .

Do I have to select a value from a lookup column?

No. If a lookup column does not display the value you want to use, you can type a different value. To hide a lookup column you displayed without selecting a value, click outside the lookup column. You can then type your own value.

Can I change the values in a lookup column?

If you want to change the values that a lookup column displays, you can recreate the lookup column. To recreate a lookup column, repeat the steps starting on page 106.

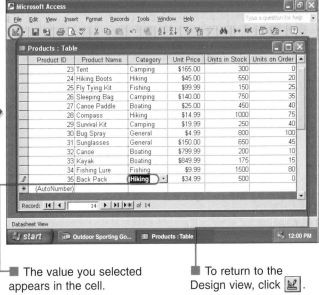

USE A LOOKUP COLUMN

1 To use a lookup column to enter data, click a cell in the field that offers the lookup column. An arrow (▼) appears.

2 Click the arrow (▼) to display the lookup column.

3 Click the value you want to enter.

■ The value you selected appears in the cell.

■ To return to the Design view, click 📐.

CREATE A YES/NO FIELD

You can create a field that accepts only one of two values—Yes/No, True/False or On/Off.

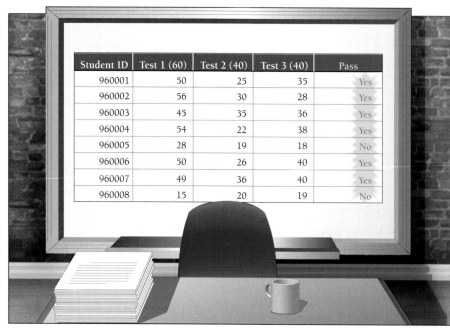

Student ID	Test 1 (60)	Test 2 (40)	Test 3 (40)	Pass
960001	50	25	35	Yes
960002	56	30	28	Yes
960003	45	35	36	Yes
960004	54	22	38	Yes
960005	28	19	18	No
960006	50	26	40	Yes
960007	49	36	40	Yes
960008	15	20	19	No

For example, you can create a Yes/No field to specify whether each student passed a course.

CREATE A YES/NO FIELD

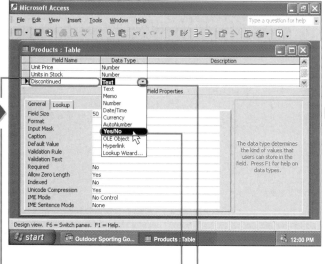

■1 Click the field you want to appear after the new Yes/No field. A triangle (▶) appears beside the field name.

■ To add a Yes/No field to the end of your table, click the area directly below the last field name. Then skip to step 3.

■2 Click ╞ to add a field to your table.

■ An area appears where you can enter information for the new field.

■3 Type a unique name for the new field and then press the Enter key.

■4 To select the data type for the new field, click the arrow (▼) in the Data Type area.

■5 Click **Yes/No**.

How can I display data in a Yes/No field?

Check Box

Displays a check box (☐).
You can click the check
box to indicate Yes (☑)
or No (☐).

Text Box

Displays a value, such as Yes
or No. You can type the value
you want to enter.

Combo Box

Displays a value, such as Yes
or No. You can type the value
you want to enter or click the
arrow (▼) in a cell to select
the value from a drop-down list.

6 To select a format for the
field, click the area beside
Format. An arrow (▼)
appears.

7 Click the arrow (▼) to
display the available formats.

8 Click the format you
want to use.

9 To select the way you
want data to appear in the
field, click the **Lookup** tab.

*Note: You can click the **General**
tab at any time to return to the
General properties.*

10 Click the area beside
Display Control. An
arrow (▼) appears.

11 Click the arrow (▼)
to display the available
options.

12 Click the display
option you want to use.

*Note: For information on the
display options, see the top
of this page.*

CONTINUED

CREATE A YES/NO FIELD

If you are creating
a Yes/No field that
uses a Combo Box,
you can specify the
values you want
to appear in the
drop-down list for
the field.

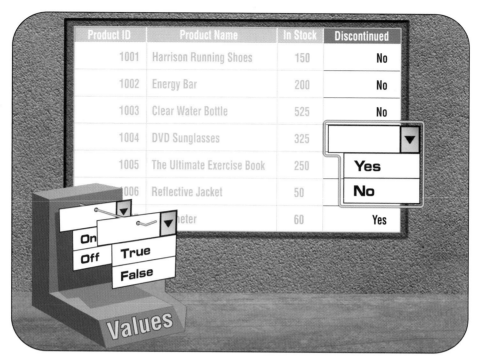

Product ID	Product Name	In Stock	Discontinued
1001	Harrison Running Shoes	150	No
1002	Energy Bar	200	No
1003	Clear Water Bottle	525	No
1004	DVD Sunglasses	325	
1005	The Ultimate Exercise Book	250	Yes
006	Reflective Jacket	50	No
	eter	60	Yes

On   True
Off   False

Values

CREATE A YES/NO FIELD (CONTINUED)

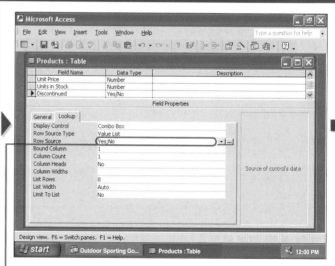

13 If you selected **Combo Box** in step **12**, click the area beside **Row Source Type**. An arrow (▾) appears.

*Note: If you selected **Check Box** or **Text Box** in step **12**, skip to step **18**.*

14 Click the arrow (▾) to display the available options.

15 Click **Value List** to be able to type the values you want to appear in the drop-down list for the field.

16 Click the area beside **Row Source**.

17 Type the two values you want to appear in the drop-down list for the field. Separate the values with a semicolon (;).

*Note: The values you type should match the format you selected in step **8**.*

How can I speed up entering data in a Yes/No field?

When you add a new record to your table, Access automatically displays the **No**, **False** or **Off** value in a Yes/No field. The value Access displays depends on the format you selected in step **8** on page 111. If most of your records will require a **Yes**, **True** or **On** value, you can change the default value to **Yes**, **True** or **On**. To set the default value for a field, see page 91.

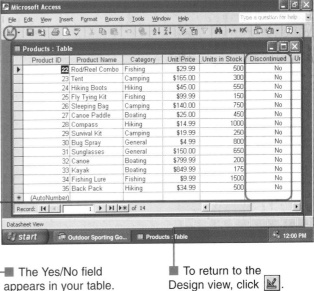

18 Click [icon] to save your changes.

19 Click [icon] to display your table in the Datasheet view.

■ The Yes/No field appears in your table.

■ To return to the Design view, click [icon].

CREATE A HYPERLINK FIELD

You can create a field that allows you to add a hyperlink to each record in a table. A hyperlink, also called a link, allows you to quickly display a Web page or file or send an e-mail message.

For example, you can create a Hyperlink field to store the Web page addresses or e-mail addresses of your suppliers. You can then select a hyperlink to quickly display a supplier's Web page or send the supplier an e-mail message.

CREATE A HYPERLINK FIELD

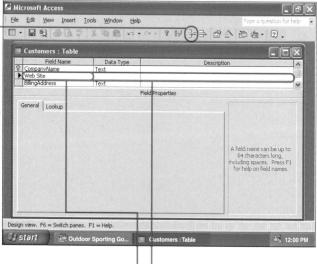

1 To create a field that will store hyperlinks, click the name of the field you want to appear after the new field. A triangle (▶) appears beside the field name.

■ To add a Hyperlink field to the end of your table, click the area directly below the last field name. Then skip to step **3**.

2 Click ∃ᶜ to add a field to your table.

■ A new row appears where you can enter information for the new field.

3 Type a unique name for the field and then press the Enter key.

What types of files can I create hyperlinks to?

You can create hyperlinks to files such as documents, pictures, spreadsheets and sounds. When you select a hyperlink to a file, the appropriate program will open and display or play the file. To select a hyperlink to a file, see page 117.

Will the Hyperlink field I add to my table appear on a form?

When you create a form using a table that contains a Hyperlink field, the form will display the Hyperlink field. You can select a hyperlink on a form as you would select a hyperlink in a table. To select a hyperlink in a table, see page 117.

4 To select the data type for the new field, click the arrow (▾) in the Data Type area.

5 Click **Hyperlink**.

6 Click 💾 to save your changes.

7 Click 🖽 to display your table in the Datasheet view.

■ The Hyperlink field appears in your table.

Note: To add hyperlinks to the field, see pages 116 to 119.

■ To return to the Design view, click 🖾.

CONTINUED

CREATE A HYPERLINK FIELD

After you create a field that will store hyperlinks, you can add hyperlinks to the field that will allow you to quickly display Web pages or files stored on your computer, network, corporate intranet or the Internet.

An intranet is a small version of the Internet within a company.

CREATE A HYPERLINK TO A WEB PAGE OR FILE

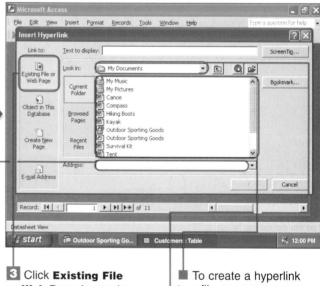

1 To create a hyperlink to a Web page or file, click the cell for the record you want to add the hyperlink to.

Note: To create a field that will store hyperlinks, see page 114.

2 Click 🔗 to add a hyperlink.

■ The Insert Hyperlink dialog box appears.

3 Click **Existing File or Web Page** to create a hyperlink to an existing file or Web page.

4 To create a hyperlink to a Web page, click this area and type the address of the Web page.

■ To create a hyperlink to a file on your computer or network, click the file in this area.

■ This area shows the location of the displayed files. You can click this area to change the location.

Is there a faster way to create a hyperlink to a Web page or file?

Yes. When you type the address of a Web page or the location and name of a file into a field that stores hyperlinks, Access will automatically change the address or location and name to a hyperlink for you.

How do I remove a hyperlink to a Web page or file?

To select the hyperlink you want to remove, position the mouse I over the left edge of the cell that contains the hyperlink (I changes to ⊕) and then click to select the contents of the cell. To delete the hyperlink, press the Delete key.

■ This area displays the text that will appear in the Hyperlink field.

5 To change the text, drag the mouse I over the text until you highlight all the text. Then type the text you want to appear in the field.

6 Click **OK** to add the hyperlink to the field.

■ Access adds the hyperlink to the field. A hyperlink appears underlined and in color.

■ When you position the mouse over a hyperlink, a yellow box appears, displaying the Web page address or the location and name of the file that the hyperlink will display.

SELECT A HYPERLINK

1 To select a hyperlink to display the Web page or file connected to the hyperlink, click the hyperlink.

CONTINUED

CREATE A HYPERLINK FIELD

After you create a field that will store hyperlinks, you can add hyperlinks to the field that will allow you to quickly send e-mail messages.

CREATE A HYPERLINK TO AN E-MAIL ADDRESS

1 To create a hyperlink to an e-mail address, click the cell for the record you want to add the hyperlink to.

Note: To create a field that will store hyperlinks, see page 114.

2 Click 🔗 to create a hyperlink.

■ The Insert Hyperlink dialog box appears.

3 Click **E-mail Address** to create a hyperlink to an e-mail address.

4 Click this area and type the e-mail address of the person you want to receive the e-mail messages.

*Note: Access automatically adds **mailto:** to the beginning of the e-mail address you type.*

5 If you want specific information to appear in the Subject area of the e-mail messages, click this area and type the subject.

Is there a faster way to create a hyperlink that will allow me to send e-mail messages?

Yes. In a field that stores hyperlinks, you can type **mailto:** followed by the e-mail address of the person you want to send messages to. For example, you can type **mailto:shawn@abccorp.com**. Access will automatically change the text you type to a hyperlink.

How do I remove a hyperlink to an e-mail address?

To select the hyperlink you want to remove, position the mouse I over the left edge of the cell that contains the hyperlink (I changes to ⬚) and then click to select the contents of the cell. To delete the hyperlink, press the Delete key.

■ This area displays the text that will appear in the Hyperlink field.

6 To change the text, drag the mouse I over the text until you highlight all the text. Then type the text you want to appear in the field.

7 Click **OK** to add the hyperlink to the field.

■ Access adds the hyperlink to the field. A hyperlink appears underlined and in color.

SELECT A HYPERLINK

1 To select a hyperlink to send an e-mail message to a person, click the hyperlink.

■ Your e-mail program will open, displaying a new message addressed to the person you specified.

119

1004	45 days	Check	Yes
1005	30 days	Check	No
1006	90 days	Check	Yes
1007	30 days	Check	
1008	30 days		

Products Table

Product ID	Product Name
6400	Bike repair kit
6401	Wet suit
6402	Lacrosse stick
6403	Leather football
6404	Skateboard
6405	Ski goggles
6406	Snowboard
6407	Surfboard
6408	T-ball stand
6409	Volleyball

ADDRESSES Table

Company ID	Company Name		City	State/Province	P
1001	Reel Fishing				
1002	Athletics Inc		Los Angeles	CA	
1003	Outer World	nd St	Cr		

Price	Units in Stock	Discontinued
	550	No
34.95	100	No
89.95	1000	No
39.95	1500	No
29.50	500	No
54.95	700	No
29.99	150	No
10.50	100	No
99.99	100	No
19.95	750	No
29.95		

ode

Establish Relationships

Do you want to establish relationships between the tables in your database? This chapter teaches you how.

SET THE PRIMARY KEY

You can set the primary key for a table. A primary key is one or more fields that uniquely identifies each record in a table. Each table in your database should have a primary key.

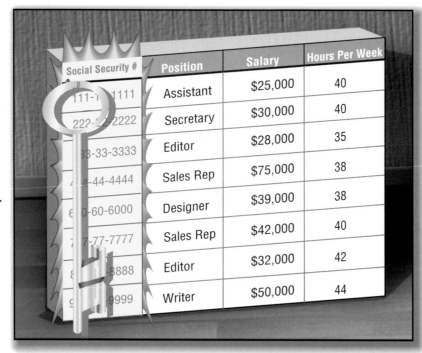

Social Security #	Position	Salary	Hours Per Week
111-11-1111	Assistant	$25,000	40
222-22-2222	Secretary	$30,000	40
33-33-3333	Editor	$28,000	35
44-44-4444	Sales Rep	$75,000	38
60-60-6000	Designer	$39,000	38
77-77-7777	Sales Rep	$42,000	40
8888	Editor	$32,000	42
9999	Writer	$50,000	44

Access uses the primary key in each table to create relationships between the tables in your database. Relationships between tables allow Access to bring together related information in the tables. For information on relationships, see page 124.

SET THE PRIMARY KEY

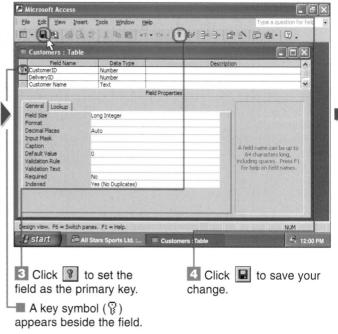

1 Display the table you want to change in the Design view. To change the view of a table, see page 74.

■ The field that is currently set as the primary key displays a key symbol (🔑).

Note: You may have had Access set a primary key for you when you created the table.

2 Click the name of the field you want to set as the primary key.

3 Click 🔑 to set the field as the primary key.

■ A key symbol (🔑) appears beside the field.

4 Click 🖫 to save your change.

What types of primary keys can I create?

AutoNumber

A field that automatically assigns a unique number to each record you add. When you create a table, Access can create an AutoNumber primary key for you.

Single-Field

A field that contains a unique value for each record, such as an invoice number, social security number or product number.

Multiple-Field

Two or more fields that together make up a unique value for each record, such as a last name and date of birth.

■ Access sets the Indexed property of the field to **Yes (No Duplicates)**. Access will index the data in the field so you can quickly sort and search for data in the field.

■ The phrase **No Duplicates** indicates that Access will not allow you to enter the same value more than once in the field.

CREATE A MULTIPLE-FIELD PRIMARY KEY

1 To set more than one field as the primary key, press and hold down the Ctrl key as you click the area to the left of each field you want to set as the primary key.

2 Click 🖋 to set the selected fields as the primary key.

■ A key symbol (🖋) appears beside each field.

CREATE RELATIONSHIPS BETWEEN TABLES

You can create relationships between tables. Relationships between tables allow you to bring together related information in your database.

Relationships between tables are essential for creating a form, query or report that uses information from more than one table in your database.

CREATE RELATIONSHIPS BETWEEN TABLES

1 Click 🖧 to display the Relationships window.

Note: If 🖧 is not available, press the **F11** *key to display the Database window.*

■ The Relationships window appears. If any relationships exist between the tables in your database, a box for each table appears in the window.

■ The Show Table dialog box may also appear, listing all the tables in your database.

2 If the Show Table dialog box does not appear, click 🔳 to display the dialog box.

Why do relationships already exist between the tables in my database?

If you used the Database Wizard to create your database, the wizard automatically created relationships between the tables for you. For information on the Database Wizard, see page 12.

How do I remove a table from the Relationships window?

To remove a table from the Relationships window, click the box for the table and then press the Delete key. Removing a table from the Relationships window will not delete the table from your database or affect the table's relationships with other tables.

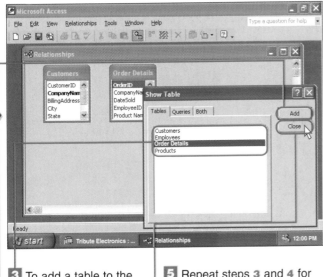

3 To add a table to the Relationships window, click the table you want to add.

4 Click **Add** to add the table to the window.

5 Repeat steps **3** and **4** for each table you want to add.

6 When you finish adding tables to the Relationships window, click **Close** to remove the Show Table dialog box.

■ Each box in the Relationships window displays the fields for one table.

■ The primary key in each table appears in **bold**. The primary key uniquely identifies each record in a table.

CONTINUED ▶

CREATE RELATIONSHIPS BETWEEN TABLES

You create a relationship between tables in your database by identifying the matching fields in the tables.

COMPANY ADDRESSES

Company ID	Company Name	Address	City	State
1	Pet Superstore	258 Linton Ave.	New York	NY
2	Petterson Inc.	50 Brittania Lane	Boston	MA
3	Martin Vet Supplies	68 Cracker Ave.	San Francisco	CA
4	Greg's Pet Store	47 Crosby Ave.	Las Vegas	NV
5	Dogs R Us	26 Arnold Cres.	Jacksonville	FL
6	Feline Foods Inc.	401 Idon Dr.	Nashville	TN
7	Weasels R Us	1320 1st Rd.	Atlanta	GA
8	Purrrrfect Portions	36 Buzzard St.	Boston	MA

ORDERS

Order ID	Company ID	Product	Quantity	Unit Price
1001	4	Vitamins	12	$20.00
1002	2	Bulk Dry Food	15	$18.00
1003	8	Diet Dog Food	30	$10.00
1004	1	5-Variety Biscuits	50	$3.50
1005	3	Canned Dog Food	24	$3.00
1006	6	Dry Cat Food	40	$4.00
1007	7	Ferret Pellets	30	$6.50
1008	5	Dry Cat Food	24	$4.00

You will usually relate the primary key in one table to a matching field in the other table. In most cases, the fields will have the same name.

The fields you use to create a relationship between tables should contain the same type of data, such as text, numbers or dates.

CREATE RELATIONSHIPS BETWEEN TABLES (CONTINUED)

7 To create a relationship between two tables, position the mouse ⌖ over a field you want to use to create the relationship.

8 Drag the field to the matching field in the other table.

■ The Edit Relationships dialog box appears.

■ This area displays the names of the tables you are creating a relationship between and the names of the matching fields.

■ This area displays the type of relationship. For information on the types of relationships, see the top of page 127.

9 Click **Create** to create the relationship.

What types of relationships can I create between tables?

One-to-One

Each record in a table relates to one record in another table. For example, each customer has only one credit record. Access creates a one-to-one relationship between tables if the matching fields are both primary keys.

One-to-Many

Each record in a table relates to one or more records in another table. This is the most common type of relationship. For example, each customer can have more than one order. Access creates a one-to-many relationship between tables if only one of the matching fields is a primary key.

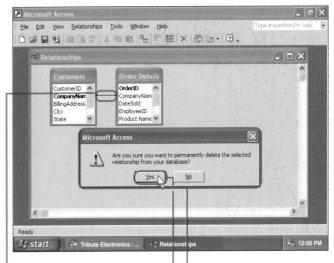

■ A line connects the fields in the two tables to show the relationship.

10 To create a relationship between other tables in your database, repeat steps **7** to **9** for each relationship you want to create.

11 Click 🖫 to save your changes.

12 When you finish working in the Relationships window, click ⊠ to close the window.

DELETE A RELATIONSHIP

1 In the Relationships window, click the line for the relationship you want to delete.

2 To delete the relationship, press the Delete key.

■ A confirmation dialog box appears.

3 Click **Yes** to permanently delete the relationship.

ENFORCE REFERENTIAL INTEGRITY

Referential integrity is a set of rules that prevents you from changing or deleting a record if matching records exist in a related table.

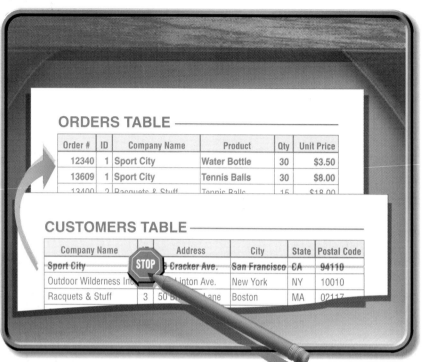

ORDERS TABLE

Order #	ID	Company Name	Product	Qty	Unit Price
12340	1	Sport City	Water Bottle	30	$3.50
13609	1	Sport City	Tennis Balls	30	$8.00
13400	2	Racquets & Stuff	Tennis Balls	15	$18.00

CUSTOMERS TABLE

Company Name		Address	City	State	Postal Code
Sport City		Cracker Ave.	San Francisco	CA	94110
Outdoor Wilderness Inc.		Linton Ave.	New York	NY	10010
Racquets & Stuff	3	50 B... Lane	Boston	MA	02117

For example, you cannot delete a customer from the Customers table if the related Orders table contains orders for the customer.

Referential integrity also prevents you from entering a record in one table if a matching record does not exist in a related table. For example, if a customer does not exist in the Customers table, you cannot enter an order for the customer in the Orders table.

ENFORCE REFERENTIAL INTEGRITY

1 Click 🔲 to display the Relationships window.

■ The Relationships window appears.

Note: If 🔲 is not available, press the **F11** *key to display the Database window.*

2 To enforce referential integrity between two tables in your database, double-click the line showing the relationship between the tables.

Note: If a line does not appear between the tables, you must create a relationship between the tables. To create a relationship, see page 124.

■ The Edit Relationships dialog box appears.

**How can I change or delete a record after I
enforce referential integrity between two tables?**

Access provides two options that allow you to
perform updating and deleting tasks that would
normally be prevented by referential integrity.

Cascade Update Related Fields

When you change data in the primary key in a
table, Access automatically updates the matching
data in the related table(s). For example, if you
change a customer ID in the Customers table,
the customer ID will automatically change for all
the customer's orders in the Orders table.

Cascade Delete Related Records

When you delete a record in a table, Access
automatically deletes matching records in the
related table(s). For example, if you delete a
customer from the Customers table, all the
customer's orders will automatically be deleted
from the Orders table.

3 Click this option to enforce
referential integrity between
the tables (☐ changes to ☑).

4 To have Access automatically
update related fields or delete
related records in the tables,
click each option you want to
use (☐ changes to ☑).

*Note: For more information
on the options, see the top
of this page.*

5 Click **OK** to confirm
your changes.

■ When you enforce
referential integrity
between two tables,
the line showing the
relationship between
the tables becomes
thicker.

■ The symbols above the line
indicate the type of relationship.
In this example, each record in
the Customers table (**1**) relates
to one or more records in the
Orders table (**∞**).

*Note: For information on the types
of relationships, see the top
of page 127.*

PivotChart

PivotTable

Create Forms

Would you like to use forms to work with data in your database? In this chapter, you will learn how to create forms to help you present data in an organized, easy-to-use format.

Which Fields
to Include?

CREATE A FORM USING AN AUTOFORM

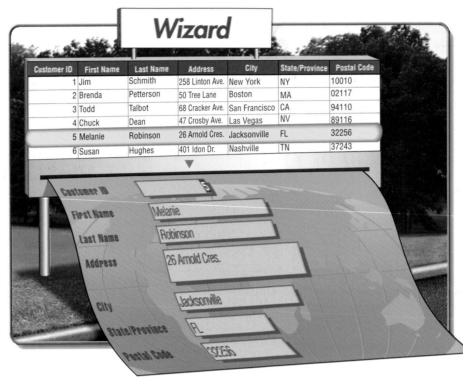

You can use the AutoForm Wizard to quickly create a form that displays the information from one table in your database.

A form presents data from a table in an attractive, easy-to-use format. You can use a form to view, enter and change data in a table.

CREATE A FORM USING AN AUTOFORM

1 Click **Forms** in the Database window.

2 Click **New** to create a new form.

■ The New Form dialog box appears.

3 Click the type of AutoForm you want to create.

Note: For information on the types of AutoForms, see the top of page 133.

4 Click ▾ to display a list of the tables in your database.

5 Click the table that contains the information you want to display on your form.

6 Click **OK** to create your form.

132

What types of AutoForms can I create?

Columnar

Displays one record at a time.

Tabular

Displays many records at a time.

Datasheet

Displays many records at a time and resembles a table in the Datasheet view.

PivotTable

Allows you to summarize and analyze data.

PivotChart

Allows you to display a graphical summary of data.

■ The form appears.

■ In this example, the form displays the field names from the table you selected and the data for the first record.

Note: If you selected PivotTable or PivotChart in step 3, the PivotTable or PivotChart initially appears empty so you must add the fields you want to display. For information on using the PivotTable or PivotChart, see pages 232 and 238.

7 Click 🖫 to save your form.

■ The Save As dialog box appears.

8 Type a name for your form and then press the Enter key.

9 When you finish reviewing the form, click ⊠ to close the form.

CREATE A FORM USING THE FORM WIZARD

You can use the Form Wizard to create a form that displays information from one or more tables in your database. The wizard asks you a series of questions and then sets up a form based on your answers.

Forms present data from tables in an attractive, easy-to-use format. You can use forms to view, enter and change data in tables.

CREATE A FORM USING THE FORM WIZARD

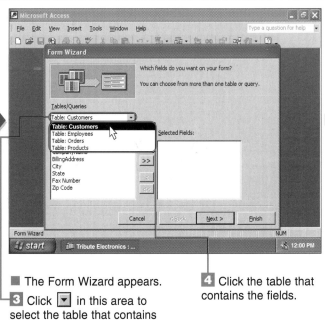

1 Click **Forms** in the Database window.

2 Double-click **Create form by using wizard**.

■ The Form Wizard appears.

3 Click ▼ in this area to select the table that contains the fields you want to include on your form.

4 Click the table that contains the fields.

Which tables in my database can I use to create a form?

You can use any table in your database to create a form. When creating a form that uses information from more than one table, relationships must exist between the tables so that Access can bring together the information in the tables. For information on relationships, see page 124.

In what order will the fields I select appear on my form?

When you select fields in the Form Wizard, the order in which you select the fields determines the order in which the fields will appear on your form. Make sure you select the fields in the order you want them to appear on your form.

■ This area displays the fields from the table you selected.

5 Double-click each field you want to include on your form.

Note: To add all the fields from the table at once, click >> .

■ Each field you select appears in this area.

6 To remove a field you accidentally selected, double-click the field in this area.

Note: To remove all the fields at once, click << .

7 To include fields from other tables in your database, repeat steps **3** to **5** for each table.

8 Click **Next** to continue.

CONTINUED ▶

CREATE A FORM USING THE FORM WIZARD

When creating a form that uses data from more than one table, you can choose the way you want to view the data on the form.

View Data Separately

View Data Together

You can choose to view the data from each table separately or together on a form.

CREATE A FORM USING THE FORM WIZARD (CONTINUED)

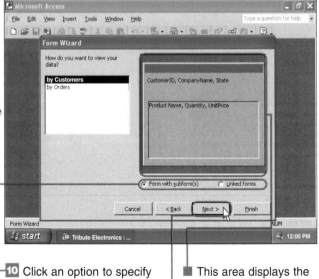

■ If you selected fields from more than one table, you can select the way you want to view the data on your form.

Note: If this screen does not appear, skip to step 12.

9 Click the way you want to view the data on your form. You can view the data from each table separately or together.

■ This area displays the way the data will appear on your form.

10 Click an option to specify if you want to create a form with a subform or a linked form (◯ changes to ⦿). For more information, see the top of page 137.

Note: If you selected to view the data from each table together in step 9, these options are not available.

■ This area displays the way the data will appear.

11 Click **Next** to continue.

136

How can I organize the data from multiple tables on a form?

If you choose to view the data from each table separately on a form, the Form Wizard offers two ways that you can organize data on the form.

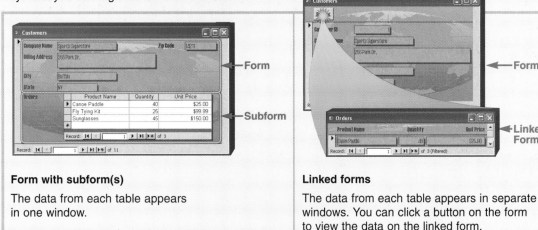

←Form

←Subform

←Form

←Linked Form

Form with subform(s)

The data from each table appears in one window.

Linked forms

The data from each table appears in separate windows. You can click a button on the form to view the data on the linked form.

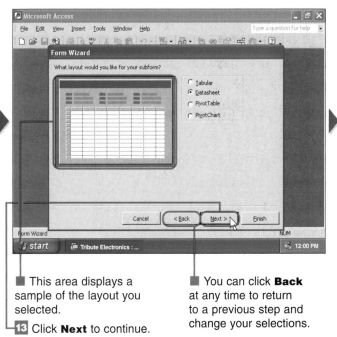

12 Click the layout you want to use for your form or subform (○ changes to ◉). For information on the available layouts, see the top of page 133.

Note: The available layout options depend on the selections you made in steps 9 and 10. If this screen does not appear, skip to step 14.

■ This area displays a sample of the layout you selected.

13 Click **Next** to continue.

■ You can click **Back** at any time to return to a previous step and change your selections.

CONTINUED

CREATE A FORM USING THE FORM WIZARD

You can choose the style you want your form to display. Access provides several styles, such as Blends, International and Ricepaper.

You may want to use the same style for every form in your database to give the database a consistent appearance.

CREATE A FORM USING THE FORM WIZARD (CONTINUED)

14 Click the style you want your form to display.

■ This area displays a sample of the style you selected.

15 Click **Next** to continue.

16 Type a name for your form.

17 If your form includes fields from more than one table, you can also specify a name for your subform or linked form. To specify a name, press the `Tab` key and then type a name for the subform or linked form.

Note: If you selected to view the data from each table together in step 9, you do not need to perform step 17.

How will my new form appear in the Database window?

The name of every form you create will appear in the Database window. If you created a form with a subform or a linked form, the subform or linked form will also appear in the Database window. You must open the main form to work with the contents of both the main form and the subform or linked form.

How do I move through the information in a subform?

When you move through the information in the main form, the information in the subform automatically changes. For example, when you display the name and address of a customer, Access automatically displays the orders for the customer in the subform. To move through records in a form, see page 141.

18 Click this option to open the form so you can review and enter information in the form (○ changes to ⊙).

19 Click **Finish** to create your form.

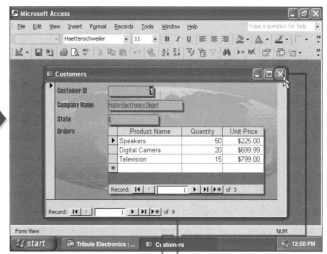

■ The form appears.

Note: The appearance of your form depends on the options you selected while creating the form.

■ In this example, the form displays the information for one customer on the main form and the orders for the customer in the subform.

20 When you finish reviewing the form, click ✕ to close the form.

OPEN A FORM

You can open a form to display its contents on your screen. Opening a form allows you to review and make changes to the form.

1 Click **Forms** in the Database window.

■ This area displays a list of the forms in your database.

2 Double-click the form you want to open.

■ The form opens. You can now review and make changes to the form.

■ When you finish working with the form, click ☒ to close the form.

Note: A dialog box will appear if you did not save changes you made to the design of the form. Click Yes or No to specify if you want to save the changes.

You can move through the records in a form to review and edit information.

MOVE THROUGH RECORDS

■ This area displays the number of the current record and the total number of records.

1 To move to another record, click one of the following buttons.

◄		First record
◄	Previous record
►	Next record
►		Last record

MOVE TO A SPECIFIC RECORD

1 To quickly move to a specific record, drag the mouse I over the number of the current record. The number is highlighted.

2 Type the number of the record you want to move to and then press the Enter key.

EDIT DATA

You can edit the data displayed on a form to correct a mistake or update data.

Access automatically saves the changes you make to the data displayed on a form.

When you change data on a form, Access will also change the data in the table you used to create the form.

EDIT DATA

INSERT DATA

1 Click the location in the cell where you want to insert data.

■ A flashing insertion point appears in the cell, indicating where the data you type will appear.

Note: You can press the ← or → key to move the insertion point.

2 Type the data you want to insert.

DELETE DATA

1 Position the mouse I to the left of the data you want to delete.

2 Drag the mouse I until you highlight all the data you want to delete.

3 Press the Delete key to delete the data.

Note: To delete a single character, click to the right of the character you want to delete and then press the ◆Backspace key.

Why does the existing data disappear when I type new data?

When **OVR** appears at the bottom right corner of your screen, the Overtype feature is on. When this feature is on, the data you type will replace the existing data. To turn off the Overtype feature, press the `Insert` key.

Why can't I edit the data in a cell?

You may be trying to edit data in a field that has the AutoNumber data type. A field that has the AutoNumber data type automatically numbers each record for you to uniquely identify each record. For more information on data types, see page 82.

REPLACE ALL DATA IN A CELL

1 To replace all the data in a cell with new data, position the mouse I over the left edge of the cell.

2 Drag the mouse I over the data until you highlight all the data in the cell.

Note: In some forms, you can click the name of the field to quickly highlight all the data in a cell.

3 Type the new data.

■ The data you type replaces the data in the cell.

UNDO CHANGES

1 Click 🔄 to immediately undo your most recent change.

Note: If you move to another cell and then click 🔄, Access will undo all the changes you made to the entire record.

143

ADD A RECORD

You can add a new record to a form to insert additional information into your database. For example, you can add information about a new customer.

Access automatically saves each new record you add to a form.

When you add a record to a form, Access also adds the record to the table you used to create the form.

ADD A RECORD

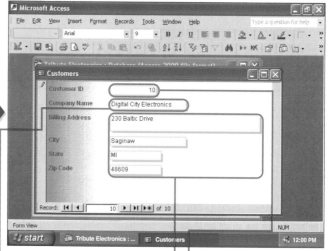

1 Click ▶* to add a new record to your form.

■ In this example, a blank form appears.

2 Click the first empty field in the form.

3 Type the data that corresponds to the field and then press the **Enter** key to move to the next field.

■ In this example, the ID field automatically adds a number for the new record.

4 Repeat step 3 until you finish entering all the data for the record.

DELETE A RECORD

You can delete a
record displayed in a
form to permanently
remove information
you no longer need.
For example, you
may want to remove
information about
a customer who no
longer orders your
products.

When you delete a
record displayed in
a form, Access also
removes the record
from the table you
used to create the
form.

Deleting records
saves storage space
on your computer
and keeps your
database from
becoming cluttered
with unnecessary
information.

DELETE A RECORD

1 Click a field in
the record you want
to delete.

2 Click ⚟ to delete
the record.

■ The record disappears
from the form.

■ A warning dialog box
appears.

3 Click **Yes** to permanently
delete the record.

RENAME A FORM

You can change the name of a form to better describe the information the form displays.

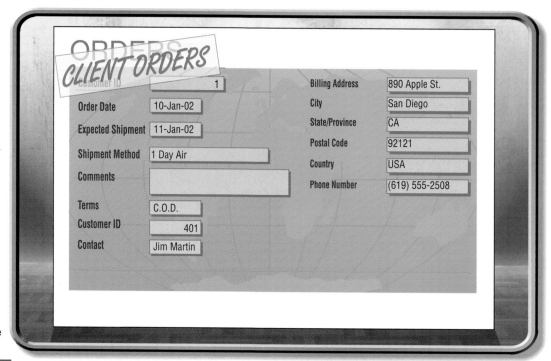

Each form in your database must have a unique name.

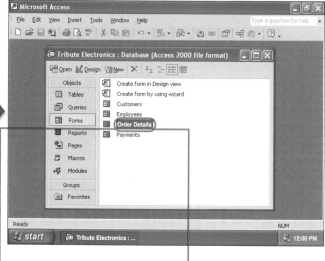

1 Click **Forms** in the Database window.

■ This area displays a list of the forms in your database.

2 Click the name of the form you want to rename.

3 After a few seconds, click the name of the form again or press the **F2** key. A black border appears around the name of the form.

Note: If you accidentally double-click the name of the form, the form will open.

4 Type a new name for the form and then press the **Enter** key.

■ The form displays the new name.

DELETE A FORM

If you no longer need a form, you can permanently delete the form from your database.

DELETE A FORM

1 Click **Forms** in the Database window.

■ This area displays a list of the forms in your database.

2 Click the name of the form you want to delete.

3 Click ✕ to delete the form.

■ A confirmation dialog box appears.

4 Click **Yes** to permanently delete the form.

■ The form disappears from the Database window.

Design Forms

Are you interested in customizing the layout and design of your forms? This chapter shows you how to move or resize items, change the appearance of data, undo changes, add a picture to a form and more.

CHANGE THE VIEW OF A FORM

You can view
a form in five
different ways.
Each view allows
you to perform
different tasks.

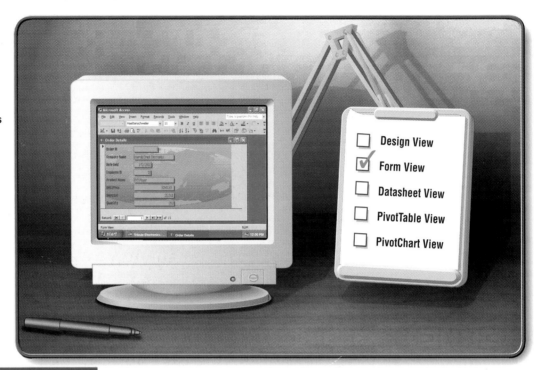

- [ ] Design View
- [x] Form View
- [ ] Datasheet View
- [ ] PivotTable View
- [ ] PivotChart View

CHANGE THE VIEW OF A FORM

■ In this example,
the form appears in
the Form view.

1 Click ⋅ in this area
to display the form in a
different view.

2 Click the view you
want to use.

■ The form appears in
the view you selected.

■ In this example, the
View button changed
from 🖳 to 🖽 .

■ To quickly switch
between the Form (🖽)
and Design (🖳) views,
click the View button.

THE FORM VIEWS

Design View

The Design view allows you to change the layout and design of a form. You can customize a form to make the form easier to use or to enhance the appearance of the form.

Form View

The Form view usually displays one record at a time in an organized and attractive format. You can use this view to review, enter and edit information.

Datasheet View

The Datasheet view displays all the records in rows and columns. The field names appear across the top of the window and the information for one record appears in each row. You can review, enter and edit information in this view.

PivotTable View

The PivotTable view allows you to summarize and analyze the data in a form. When you first display a form in this view, the PivotTable is empty and you must add the fields you want the PivotTable to display. For information on using the PivotTable view, see page 232.

PivotChart View

The PivotChart view allows you to display a graphical summary of the data in a form. When you first display a form in this view, the PivotChart is empty and you must add the fields you want the PivotChart to display. For information on using the PivotChart view, see page 238.

MOVE OR RESIZE A CONTROL

You can change the location and size of a control on a form.

Moving a control allows you to change the order of information on a form. Resizing a control allows you to display more or less information in a control.

A control is an item on a form, such as a label that displays a field name or a text box that displays data from a field.

MOVE A CONTROL

1 Display the form you want to change in the Design view. To change the view of a form, see page 150.

2 Click the control you want to move. Handles (■) appear around the control.

3 Position the mouse ⌖ over the border of the control (⌖ changes to ✋) and then drag the control to a new location on the form.

■ In this example, the label and corresponding text box appear in the new location.

4 Click 🖫 to save your change.

■ To move a label or text box individually, perform steps **1** to **3**, except position the mouse ⌖ over the large handle (■) at the top left corner of the control in step **3** (⌖ changes to ✋).

152

How can I quickly resize a label to fit its contents?

1 Click the label you want to resize to fit its contents.

2 Click **Format**.

3 Click **Size**.

4 Click **To Fit**.

How can I make small changes to the size of a control?

To make small changes to the size of a control, click the control you want to resize and then press and hold down the Shift key as you press the ↑, ↓, ← or → key.

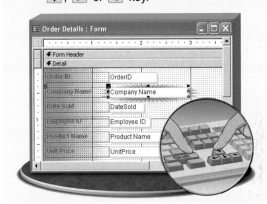

RESIZE A CONTROL

1 Display the form you want to change in the Design view. To change the view of a form, see page 150.

2 Click the control you want to resize. Handles (■) appear around the control.

3 Position the mouse ⟋ over a handle (⟋ changes to ↔, ↕, ↖ or ↗) and then drag the handle until the control is the size you want.

■ The control appears in the new size.

4 Click 🖫 to save your change.

DELETE A CONTROL

You can delete a control you no longer want to appear on a form.

A control is an item on a form, such as a label that displays a field name or a text box that displays data from a field.

DELETE A CONTROL

■1 Display the form you want to change in the Design view. To change the view of a form, see page 150.

■2 To delete a text box and its corresponding label, click the text box. Handles (■) appear around the text box.

■ To delete only a label, click the label. Handles (■) appear around the label.

■3 Press the Delete key.

■ In this example, the text box and its corresponding label disappear.

■4 Click 🖫 to save your change.

154

CHANGE THE SIZE OF A FORM

You can change the
size of an entire
form. Increasing the
size of a form can
give you more room
to add information
such as a new field
or a picture.

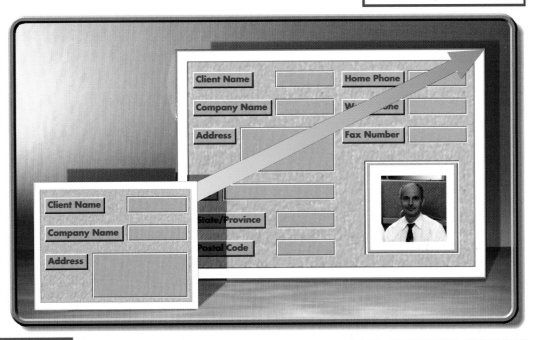

CHANGE THE SIZE OF A FORM

1 Display the form you
want to change in the
Design view. To change
the view of a form, see
page 150.

2 Position the mouse ⌖
over the right or bottom
edge of the form (⌖ changes
to ↔ or ↕).

3 Drag the edge of the
form to the size you want.

■ The form changes
to the new size.

4 Click 🖫 to save your
change.

ADD A FIELD

You can add a field to a form when you want the form to display additional information.

For example, you may want to add a Telephone Number field to a form that displays customer addresses.

Adding a field to a form is useful if you did not include all the fields from a table when you created a form.

ADD A FIELD

1 Display the form you want to change in the Design view. To change the view of a form, see page 150.

2 Click 🖳 to display a list of fields from the table you used to create the form.

3 Position the mouse ⬚ over the field you want to add to your form.

4 Drag the field to where you want the field to appear on your form.

■ The label and corresponding text box for the field appear on your form.

Note: To move or resize the label or text box, see page 152.

5 Click 🖫 to save your change.

6 To hide the box displaying the list of fields, click ☒.

ADD A LABEL

You can add a label that you want to appear for each record on a form. Labels are useful for displaying important information.

ADD A LABEL

1 Display the form you want to change in the Design view. To change the view of a form, see page 150.

2 Click on the Toolbox toolbar to add a label to your form.

■ If the Toolbox toolbar is not displayed, click ⚒ to display the toolbar.

3 Click the location on your form where you want the top left corner of the label to appear.

4 Type the text for the label and then press the **Enter** key.

5 Click 🖫 to save your change.

Note: To move or resize the label, see page 152.

■ To delete a label from a form, click the label and then press the **Delete** key.

157

CHANGE LABEL TEXT

You can change the text displayed in a label to make the label more descriptive.

You should not change the text in a text box. This text tells Access where to find the information that will appear in the text box.

CHANGE LABEL TEXT

1 Display the form you want to change in the Design view. To change the view of a form, see page 150.

2 Click the label you want to change.

3 To select all the text in the label, position the mouse I over the left edge of the label.

4 Drag the mouse I until you highlight all the text in the label.

5 Type the new text for the label and then press the Enter key.

6 Click 🖫 to save your change.

You can bold, italicize or underline data on a form to emphasize information.

BOLD, ITALICIZE OR UNDERLINE DATA

1 Display the form you want to change in the Design view. To change the view of a form, see page 150.

2 Click the control that displays the data you want to bold, italicize or underline.

3 Click one of the following buttons.

B Bold

I Italic

U Underline

■ The data in the control appears in the new style.

Note: If the control is not large enough to display all the data, you can increase the size of the control. To resize a control, see page 152.

4 Click 🖫 to save your change.

■ To remove a bold, italic or underline style from data, repeat steps **1** to **4**.

CHANGE THE FONT OF DATA

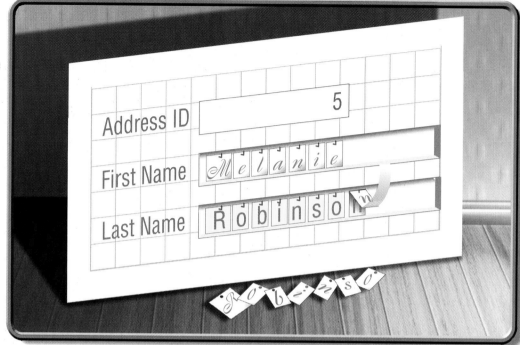

You can change the font of data in a control to enhance the appearance of a form.

A control is an item on a form, such as a label that displays a field name or a text box that displays data from a field.

CHANGE THE FONT OF DATA

1 Display the form you want to change in the Design view. To change the view of a form, see page 150.

2 Click the control that displays the data you want to change to a different font.

3 Click ▼ in this area to display a list of the available fonts.

4 Click the font you want to use.

■ The data changes to the font you selected.

Note: If the control is not large enough to display all the data, you can increase the size of the control. To resize a control, see page 152.

5 Click 🖫 to save your change.

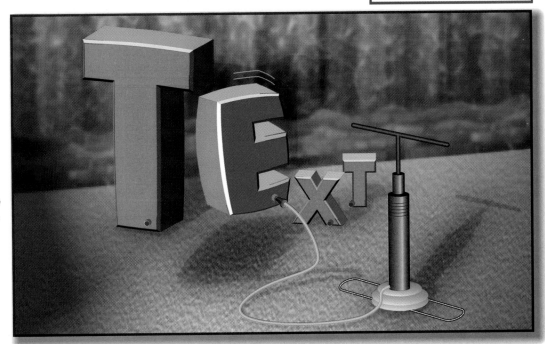

You can increase or decrease the size of data in a control.

Access measures the size of data in points. There are 72 points in an inch.

A control is an item on a form, such as a label that displays a field name or a text box that displays data from a field.

CHANGE THE SIZE OF DATA

1 Display the form you want to change in the Design view. To change the view of a form, see page 150.

2 Click the control that displays the data you want to change to a new size.

3 Click ▼ in this area to display a list of the available sizes.

4 Click the size you want to use.

■ The data changes to the size you selected.

Note: If the control is not large enough to display all the data, you can increase the size of the control. To resize a control, see page 152.

5 Click 🖬 to save your change.

CHANGE THE COLOR OF A CONTROL

You can change the background color and text color of a control to emphasize information on a form.

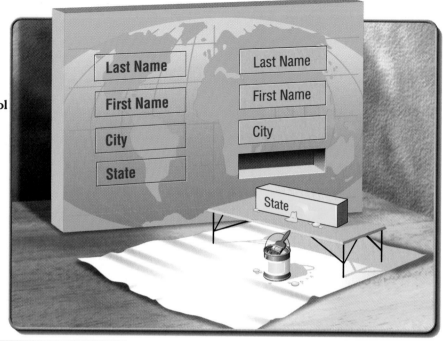

Make sure you select background and text colors that work well together. For example, red text on a blue background can be difficult to read.

A control is an item on a form, such as a label that displays a field name or a text box that displays data from a field.

CHANGE THE BACKGROUND COLOR

1 Display the form you want to change in the Design view. To change the view of a form, see page 150.

2 Click the control you want to change to a different background color.

3 Click ⊡ in this area to display the available background colors.

4 Click the background color you want to use.

■ The control displays the background color you selected.

5 Click 🖫 to save your change.

Can I change the color of several controls at once?

Yes. To select each control you want to change to a different color, hold down the Shift key as you click each control. Handles (■) appear around each control you select. To select the background color or text color you want to use, perform steps **3** and **4** below.

How can I quickly reapply the last color I used?

The Fill Color (🖌) and Font Color (A) buttons show the last background and text color you used. To reapply the last background or text color you used, click the control you want to change to a different color and then click the Fill Color (🖌) or Font Color (A) button.

CHANGE THE TEXT COLOR

1 Display the form you want to change in the Design view. To change the view of a form, see page 150.

2 Click the control that displays the text you want to change to a different color.

3 Click 🔽 in this area to display the available text colors.

4 Click the text color you want to use.

■ The text in the control displays the color you selected.

5 Click 🖫 to save your change.

CHANGE THE ALIGNMENT OF DATA

You can align data on a form in three different ways.

- Right
- Center
- Left

When a form is displayed in the Form view, Access automatically left aligns text and right aligns numbers and dates on the form.

Order ID	**1**
Date Sold	1/12/2002
Quantity	350
Unit Price	$299.99
Product Name	DVD Player
Company Name	Emerald Creek Electronics

CHANGE THE ALIGNMENT OF DATA

1 Display the form you want to change in the Design view. To change the view of a form, see page 150.

Note: When a form is displayed in the Design view, all data initially appears left aligned.

2 Click the control that displays the data you want to align differently.

3 Click one of the following buttons.

- ▤ Left align
- ▤ Center
- ▤ Right align

◾ The data in the control appears in the alignment you selected.

4 Click 🖫 to save your change.

Access remembers the last changes you made to a form. If you regret these changes, you can cancel them by using the Undo feature.

Access can only undo changes you made since you last opened the form.

UNDO CHANGES

1 When working with a form in the Design view, click to undo the last change you made to your form.

Note: To change the view of a form, see page 150.

■ Access cancels the last change you made to your form in the Design view.

■ You can repeat step 1 to cancel previous changes you made to your form in the Design view.

■ To reverse the results of using the Undo feature, click .

ADD A PICTURE

You can add a picture to a form to make the form more appealing or to help illustrate your data.

You can add a picture such as your company logo, a colorful design or a picture of your products.

If you want to display a different picture for each record, such as a picture of each employee, see page 102.

ADD A PICTURE

1 Display the form you want to add a picture to in the Design view. To change the view of a form, see page 150.

2 Click ■ on the Toolbox toolbar to add a picture to your form.

■ If the Toolbox toolbar is not displayed, click 🛠 to display the toolbar.

3 Click the location on your form where you want the top left corner of the picture to appear.

■ The Insert Picture dialog box appears.

Where can I obtain pictures that I can add to my forms?

You can use a drawing program to create your own pictures or use a scanner to scan existing pictures into your computer. You can also buy a collection of pictures, called clip art, at most computer stores. Many pages on the Web also offer pictures that you can use.

How can I delete a picture I added to a form?

To delete a picture you no longer want to appear on a form, click the picture and then press the Delete key. Access will remove the picture from the form, but will not remove the original picture from your computer.

■ This area shows the location of the displayed pictures. You can click this area to change the location.

4 Click the name of the picture you want to add to your form.

5 Click **OK** to add the picture to your form.

■ The picture appears on your form.

6 Click 🖫 to save your change.

Note: To move or resize the picture, see page 152.

APPLY CONDITIONAL FORMATTING

You can have Access apply special formatting to data in a field when the data meets a condition you specify. Applying conditional formatting to data in a field allows you to easily monitor data of interest.

For example, when the number of units in stock for a product falls below 10, you can have the number appear in red.

INVENTORY

Product	In Stock	Product	In Stock
Life Jackets	19	Sleeping Bags	108
Canoe Paddles	135	Tents	7
Boat Cushions	23	Compasses	54
Bailing Buckets	8	Emergency Whistles	3
Fishing Rods	120	Portable Stoves	33

APPLY CONDITIONAL FORMATTING

1 Click anywhere in the field that displays the data you want to apply conditional formatting to.

2 Click **Format**.

3 Click **Conditional Formatting**.

■ The Conditional Formatting dialog box appears.

■ This area displays how the data currently appears in the field.

4 Click this area to select the operator you want to use to specify the data you want to apply conditional formatting to.

5 Click the operator you want to use.

6 Click this area and then type the value that specifies the data you want to apply conditional formatting to.

What operators can I use?

Operator	Result
between 100 and 200	Formats data between 100 and 200.
not between 100 and 200	Formats data not between 100 and 200.
equal to 100	Formats data equal to 100.
not equal to 100	Formats data not equal to 100.
greater than 100	Formats data greater than 100.
less than 100	Formats data less than 100.
greater than or equal to 100	Formats data greater than or equal to 100.
less than or equal to 100	Formats data less than or equal to 100.

How do I remove conditional formatting from a field?

In the Conditional Formatting dialog box, click **Delete**. In the Delete Conditional Format dialog box that appears, click **Condition 1** (☐ changes to ☑) and then press the Enter key.

7 If you selected **between** or **not between** in step **5**, click this area and type the second value.

8 To add a background color to data that meets the condition you specified, click ⬇ in this area.

9 Click the background color you want to use.

10 To change the color of data that meets the condition you specified, you can repeat steps **8** and **9** in this area.

11 To bold (**B**), italicize (*I*) or underline (u) data that meets the condition you specified, click the appropriate button.

■ This area displays how the data that meets the condition you specified will appear on your form.

12 Click **OK** to confirm your changes.

■ When data in the field meets the condition you specified, the data will display the format you specified.

APPLY AN AUTOFORMAT

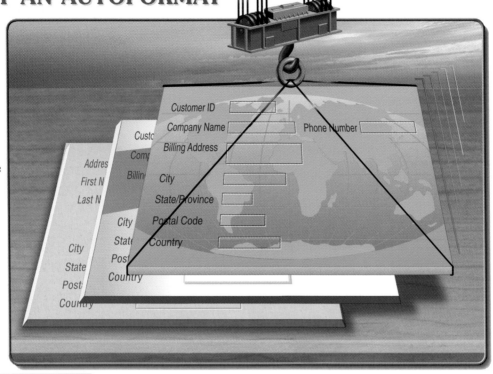

You can apply an autoformat to quickly change the overall appearance of a form.

You may want to use the same autoformat for every form in your database to give your database a consistent appearance.

1 Display the form you want to change in the Design view. To change the view of a form, see page 150.

2 Click ☐ to select the form (☐ changes to ▪).

3 Click 📷 to select an autoformat for the form.

■ The AutoFormat dialog box appears.

**Why didn't my entire form change
to the new autoformat?**

If your form contains a subform,
the appearance of the subform
will not change when you apply an
autoformat to the form. A subform
displays information from a related
table in your database. To apply
an autoformat to a subform, open
the subform as you would open
any form and then perform the
steps shown below. To open a
form, see page 140.

*Note: If your subform appears in the
Datasheet layout, applying an autoformat
to the subform will have no effect on the
appearance of the subform.*

Subform

4 Click the autoformat
you want to use.

■ This area displays a
sample of the autoformat
you selected.

5 Click **OK** to confirm
your change.

■ The form displays
the new autoformat.

6 Click 🖫 to save
your change.

Find Data

Do you often need to find specific data in your database? In this chapter, you will learn how to sort, find, replace and filter data.

	Title	Year Published	Pages
2001	360 g in Orbit	2001	360
2	Escape from Reality	1990	400
3	Hugh's Haunted Castle	1994	315
4	Still Waters Run Deep	1996	375
2001	545 urist	2001	545
6	The Cowboy Invasion	1993	250
7	My Clandestine Ways	1991	325
2001	425 cal Lilac Tree	2001	425

SORT RECORDS

You can change the order of records in a table, form or in the results of a query. Sorting records can help you find, organize and analyze data.

SORT RECORDS

SORT BY ONE FIELD

1 Click anywhere in the field you want to use to sort the records.

2 Click one of the following buttons.

- ↓ Sort A to Z, 1 to 9
- ↓ Sort Z to A, 9 to 1

■ The records appear in the new order. In this example, the records are sorted by payment amount.

How do I remove a sort from my records?

After sorting records, you can return your records to the original sort order at any time.

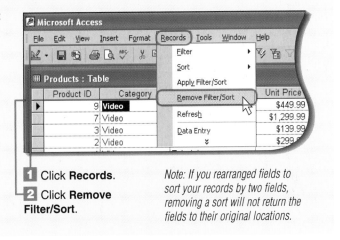

1 Click **Records**.

2 Click **Remove Filter/Sort**.

Note: If you rearranged fields to sort your records by two fields, removing a sort will not return the fields to their original locations.

SORT BY TWO FIELDS

1 Place the fields you want to use to sort the records side by side and in the order you want to perform the sort. Access will sort the leftmost field first. To rearrange fields, see page 43.

2 Position the mouse I over the name of the first field you want to use to sort the records (I changes to ↓). Then drag the mouse ↓ until you highlight the second field.

3 Click one of the following buttons.

↓ Sort A to Z, 1 to 9
↓ Sort Z to A, 9 to 1

■ The records appear in the new order. In this example, the records are sorted by payment method. All records with the same payment method are also sorted by payment amount.

FIND DATA

You can search for data of interest in a table, form or in the results of a query.

FIND DATA

1 Click anywhere in the field that contains the data you want to find.

2 Click 🔍 to find the data.

■ The Find and Replace dialog box appears.

3 Type the data you want to find.

4 To specify how you want to search for the data, click this area.

5 Click the way you want to search for the data.

Note: For information on the ways you can search for data, see the top of page 177.

How can I search for data in a field?

Any Part of Field

Finds data anywhere in a field. For example, a search for **smith** finds **Smith**, **Smithson** and **Macsmith**.

Whole Field

Finds data that exactly matches the data you specify. For example, a search for **smith** finds **Smith**, but not **Smithson** or **Macsmith**.

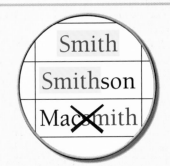

Start of Field

Finds data only at the beginning of a field. For example, a search for **smith** finds **Smith** and **Smithson**, but not **Macsmith**.

6 Click **Find Next** to start the search.

■ Access highlights the first instance of matching data in the field.

■ If the Find and Replace dialog box covers the highlighted data, position the mouse � over the title bar and then drag the dialog box to a new location.

7 Click **Find Next** to find the next instance of matching data in the field.

8 Repeat step **7** until a dialog box appears, telling you the search is complete.

9 Click **OK** to close the dialog box.

10 To close the Find and Replace dialog box, click **Cancel**.

REPLACE DATA

You can find and replace data in a table, form or in the results of a query. The Replace feature is useful when you want to make the same change to many records.

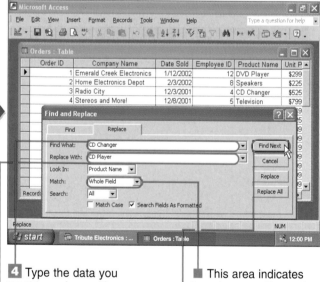

1 Click anywhere in the field that contains the data you want to replace with new data.

2 Click **Edit**.

3 Click **Replace**.

Note: If Replace does not appear on the menu, position the mouse ⌖ over the bottom of the menu to display all the menu options.

■ The Find and Replace dialog box appears.

4 Type the data you want to replace with new data.

5 Click this area and type the new data.

■ This area indicates how Access will search for the data. You can click this area to change how Access will search for the data. For more information, see the top of page 177.

6 Click **Find Next** to start the search.

How do I move the Find and Replace dialog box?

To move the Find and Replace dialog box so you can clearly view the data in your table, form or query, position the mouse over the title bar of the dialog box and then drag the dialog box to a new location.

How can the Replace feature help me quickly enter data?

You can type a short form of a word or phrase, such as MA, when entering data in a field. You can then use the Replace feature to replace the short form with the full word or phrase, such as Massachusetts.

■ Access highlights the first instance of matching data in the field.

7 Click one of the following options.

Find Next - Skip the data and find the next instance of matching data in the field.

Replace - Replace the data.

Replace All - Replace the data and all other instances of matching data in the field.

*Note: If you select **Replace All**, a dialog box will appear. Click **Yes** to continue.*

■ In this example, Access replaces the data and searches for the next instance of matching data in the field.

8 Repeat step 7 until a dialog box appears, telling you the search is complete.

9 Click **OK** to close the dialog box.

10 To close the Find and Replace dialog box, click **Cancel**.

FILTER BY SELECTION

You can filter records in a table, form or in the results of a query to display only the records that contain data of interest. Filtering records can help you review and analyze information in your database.

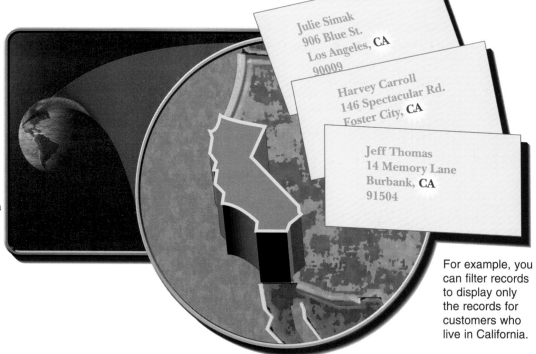

For example, you can filter records to display only the records for customers who live in California.

FILTER BY SELECTION

1 Click the data you want to use to filter the records. Access will display only the records that contain exactly the same data.

Note: You can select data to change the way Access filters records. For more information, see the top of page 181.

2 Click 🍸 to filter the records.

■ Access displays only the records that contain the same data. All other records are temporarily hidden.

■ In this example, Access displays only the employees in the Sales department.

180

How can I change the way Access filters records?

You can select data to change the way Access
filters records. To select data, see page 55.

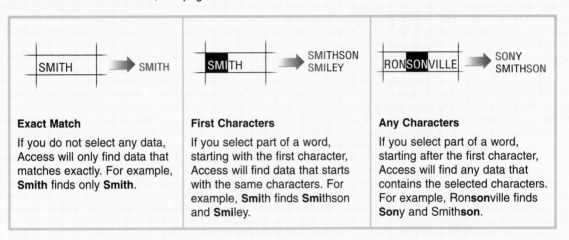

Exact Match

If you do not select any data,
Access will only find data that
matches exactly. For example,
Smith finds only **Smith**.

First Characters

If you select part of a word,
starting with the first character,
Access will find data that starts
with the same characters. For
example, **Smi**th finds **Smi**thson
and **Smi**ley.

Any Characters

If you select part of a word,
starting after the first character,
Access will find any data that
contains the selected characters.
For example, Ron**son**ville finds
Sony and Smith**son**.

■ The word **Filtered**
appears in this area to
indicate that you are
viewing filtered records.

■ To further filter
the records, you can
repeat steps 1 and 2.

3 When you finish
reviewing the filtered
records, click ▽ to
once again display
all the records.

FILTER BY INPUT

You can filter records in a table, form or in the results of a query by entering criteria. Criteria are conditions that identify which records you want to display.

For example, you can enter criteria to display only the records for customers who made purchases of more than $500.

FILTER BY INPUT

1 Right-click anywhere in the field you want to use to filter the records. A menu appears.

2 Click the area beside **Filter For:**.

3 Type the criteria you want to use to filter the records. Then press the `Enter` key.

Note: For examples of criteria you can use, see page 185.

■ Access displays only the records that meet the criteria you specified. All other records are temporarily hidden.

■ In this example, Access displays orders over $300.

■ The word **Filtered** appears in this area to indicate that you are viewing filtered records.

4 When you finish reviewing the filtered records, click ▽ to once again display all the records.

You can filter
records in a table,
form or in the
results of a query
to hide records
that do not contain
data of interest.

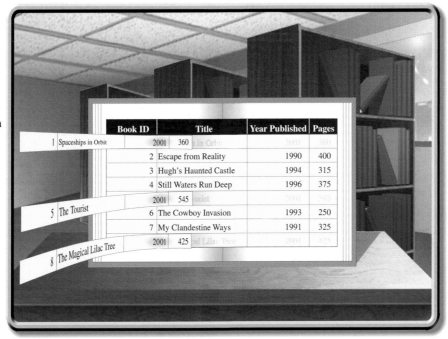

For example,
you can filter
records to hide
the records
for all books
published
in 2001.

FILTER BY EXCLUSION

1 Click the data you
want to use to filter the
records. Access will hide
all records that contain
exactly the same data.

2 Click **Records**.

3 Click **Filter**.

4 Click **Filter Excluding
Selection**.

■ Access temporarily hides
the records that contain the
data you specified.

■ In this example, Access
hides the employees in the
Sales department.

■ The word **Filtered** appears
in this area to indicate that you
are viewing filtered records.

■ To further filter the
records, you can repeat
steps **1** to **4**.

5 When you finish
reviewing the filtered
records, click ▽ to
once again display all
the records.

FILTER BY FORM

You can use the Filter by Form feature to find and display records of interest in a table, form or in the results of a query.

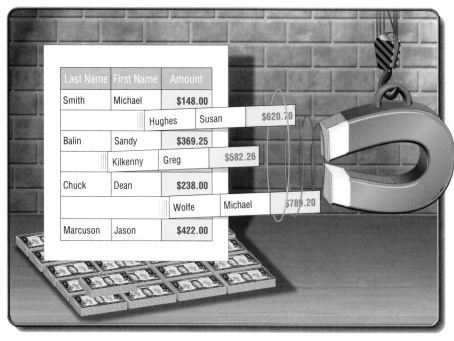

When you filter by form, you need to specify the criteria that records must meet to appear in the results. For example, you can specify criteria to display only the records for customers who purchased more than $500 of your products.

FILTER BY FORM USING ONE CRITERIA

1 Click 🔽 to filter your records by form.

■ The Filter by Form window appears.

■ This area displays the field names from your table, form or query results.

2 To clear any information used for your last filter, click ☒.

What criteria can I use to filter records?

Here are some examples of criteria you can use to filter records. For more examples, see page 212.

Criteria	Description
<100	Less than 100
>100	Greater than 100
=Texas	Matches Texas
Between 100 and 200	Between 100 and 200
Like Mar*	Starts with "Mar"
Like *mar*	Contains "mar"

Is there another way to enter the criteria I want to use to filter records?

Yes. To enter criteria, you can perform steps **1** to **3** below and then click the arrow (▼) that appears in the area. A list of all the values in the field appears. Click the value you want to use to filter the records.

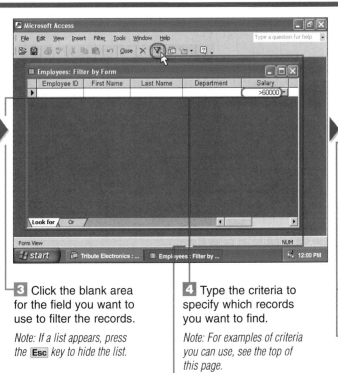

3 Click the blank area for the field you want to use to filter the records.

Note: If a list appears, press the Esc key to hide the list.

4 Type the criteria to specify which records you want to find.

Note: For examples of criteria you can use, see the top of this page.

5 Click ⟨Y⟩ to filter the records.

■ Access displays only the records that meet the criteria you specified.

■ In this example, Access displays employees who earn more than $60,000.

■ The word **Filtered** appears in this area to indicate that you are viewing filtered records.

6 When you finish reviewing the filtered records, click ⟨Y⟩ to once again display all the records.

CONTINUED ▶

FILTER BY FORM

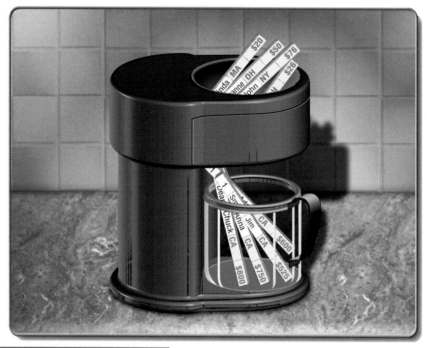

When using the Filter by Form feature, you can use multiple criteria to filter your records. Access will find and display records that meet the criteria you specify.

Criteria are conditions that identify which records you want to appear in the results. For example, you can specify criteria to display customers living in California who purchased more than $500 of your products. For more examples of criteria, see page 212.

FILTER BY FORM USING MULTIPLE CRITERIA

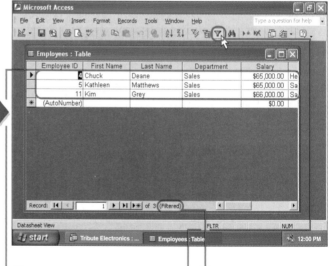

USING "AND"

■1 To enter the first criteria you want to use to filter the records, perform steps 1 to 4 starting on page 184.

■2 To enter the second criteria, click the blank area for the other field you want to use to filter the records. Then type the second criteria.

■3 Click ▼ to filter the records.

■ Access displays the records that meet both of the criteria you specified.

■ In this example, Access displays employees in the Sales department who earn more than $60,000.

■ The word **Filtered** appears in this area to indicate that you are viewing filtered records.

■4 When you finish reviewing the filtered records, click ▼ to once again display all the records.

How can I use multiple criteria to filter records?

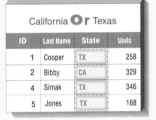

Filter records using "And"

Displays records that meet all of the criteria you specify. For example, **Texas and >200** displays only customers living in Texas who purchased more than 200 units.

Filter records using "Or"

Displays records that meet at least one of the criteria you specify. For example, **California or Texas** displays customers who live in California or Texas.

USING "OR"

1 To enter the first criteria you want to use to filter the records, perform steps **1** to **4** starting on page 184.

2 Click the **Or** tab.

3 To enter the second criteria, click the blank area for the field you want to use to filter the records. Then type the second criteria.

4 Click ▽ to filter the records.

■ Access displays the records that meet at least one of the criteria you specified.

■ In this example, Access displays employees in the Sales or Accounting department.

■ The word **Filtered** appears in this area to indicate that you are viewing filtered records.

5 When you finish reviewing the filtered records, click ▽ to once again display all the records.

Create Queries

Would you like to create queries to find information of interest in your database? This chapter shows you how.

CREATE A QUERY IN THE DESIGN VIEW

You can create a query to find information of interest in your database.

Creating a query allows you to find information that meets certain criteria in your database. Criteria are conditions that identify which records you want to find.

Which wines were made before 1965?

CREATE A QUERY IN THE DESIGN VIEW

1 Click **Queries** in the Database window.

2 Double-click **Create query in Design view**.

■ The Select Query window and the Show Table dialog box appear.

■ This area lists all the tables in your database.

3 Click a table that contains information you want to use in your query.

4 Click **Add** to add the table to your query.

Why does a line appear between the tables in the Select Query window?

If the tables you select to use in a query are related, Access displays a line joining the related fields in the tables. When creating a query that uses information from more than one table, the tables should be related so that Access can bring together the information in the tables. For information on relationships, see page 124.

How do I add another table to my query?

To add another table to your query, click 🔲 to redisplay the Show Table dialog box. Then perform steps **3** and **4** on page 190 to add another table to your query.

■ A box appears in the Select Query window, displaying the fields for the table you selected.

5 To add another table to your query, repeat steps **3** and **4** for each table.

6 Click **Close** to hide the Show Table dialog box.

■ Each box in this area displays the fields for one table.

■ If you accidentally added a table to the query, click the box displaying the fields for the table and then press the Delete key. Access will remove the table from the query, but will not remove the table from the database.

CONTINUED

CREATE A QUERY IN THE DESIGN VIEW

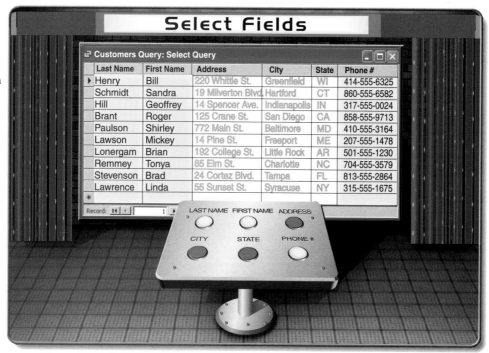

You can select which fields from your tables you want to include in your query.

Select Fields

For example, you may want to include only the name and phone number of each customer.

CREATE A QUERY IN THE DESIGN VIEW (CONTINUED)

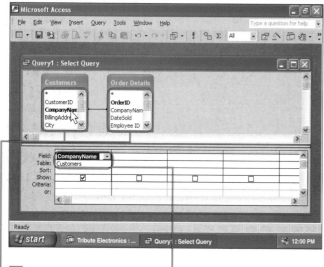

7 Double-click a field you want to include in your query.

■ This area displays the field you selected and the table that contains the field.

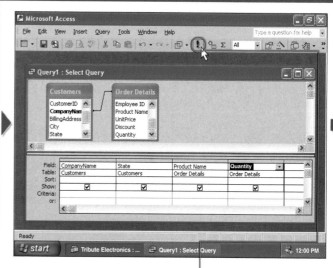

8 To include other fields in your query, repeat step **7** for each field you want to include.

Note: To quickly select all the fields in a table, see page 204.

RUN A QUERY

1 Click [!] to run the query.

Does a query store data?

No. When you save a query, Access saves only the design of the query. Each time you run a query, Access gathers the most current data from your database to determine the results of the query. For example, you can run the same query each month to display the top sales representatives for the month.

Can I change information displayed in the results of my query?

Yes. You can edit data displayed in the results of a query as you would edit data in a table. If you change the data displayed in the query results, the data will also change in the table used to create the query. To edit data in a table, see page 56.

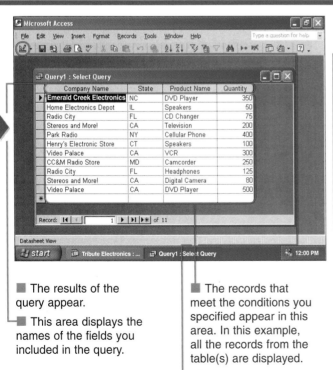

■ The results of the query appear.

■ This area displays the names of the fields you included in the query.

■ The records that meet the conditions you specified appear in this area. In this example, all the records from the table(s) are displayed.

■ To return to the Design view, click 📐.

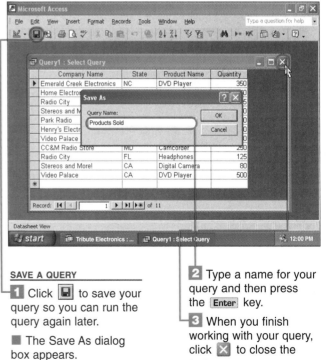

SAVE A QUERY

1 Click 💾 to save your query so you can run the query again later.

■ The Save As dialog box appears.

2 Type a name for your query and then press the **Enter** key.

3 When you finish working with your query, click ✕ to close the query.

CREATE A QUERY USING THE SIMPLE QUERY WIZARD

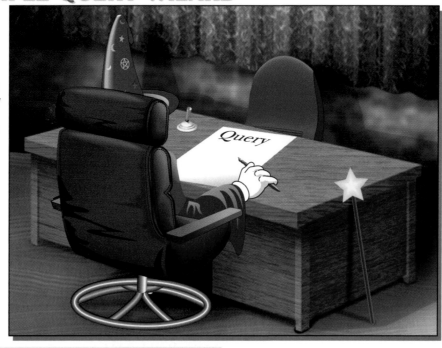

You can use the Simple Query Wizard to create a query. A query allows you to find and analyze information of interest in your database.

The Simple Query Wizard will ask you a series of questions and then set up a query based on your answers.

CREATE A QUERY USING THE SIMPLE QUERY WIZARD

1 Click **Queries** in the Database window.

2 Double-click **Create query by using wizard**.

■ The Simple Query Wizard appears.

3 Click ▼ in this area to select the table that contains the fields you want to include in your query.

4 Click the table that contains the fields.

TEACH YOURSELF
TY

Which tables in my database can I use to create a query?

You can use any table in your database to create a query. When creating a query that uses information from more than one table, relationships must exist between the tables so that Access can bring together the information in the tables. For information on relationships, see page 124.

■ This area displays the fields from the table you selected.

5 Double-click each field you want to include in your query.

Note: To add all the fields from the table at once, click >> .

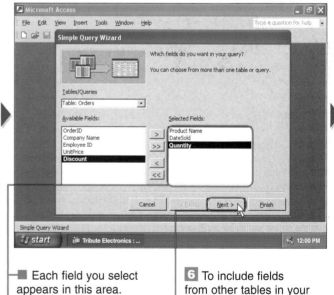

■ Each field you select appears in this area.

■ To remove a field you accidentally selected, double-click the field in this area.

Note: To remove all the fields at once, click << .

6 To include fields from other tables in your database, repeat steps **3** to **5** for each table.

7 Click **Next** to continue.

CONTINUED ▶

CREATE A QUERY USING THE SIMPLE QUERY WIZARD

If your query contains information that Access can summarize, you can choose to show all the records or just a summary of the records in the results of your query.

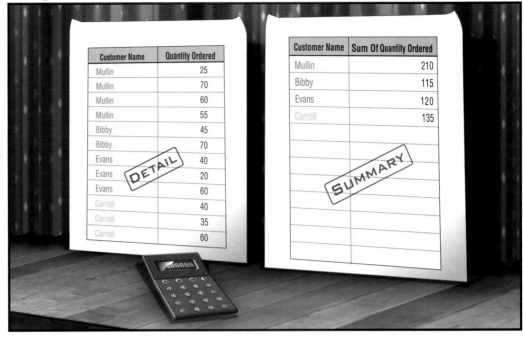

Customer Name	Quantity Ordered
Mullin	25
Mullin	70
Mullin	60
Mullin	55
Bibby	45
Bibby	70
Evans	40
Evans	20
Evans	60
Carroll	40
Carroll	35
Carroll	60

DETAIL

Customer Name	Sum Of Quantity Ordered
Mullin	210
Bibby	115
Evans	120
Carroll	135

SUMMARY

CREATE A QUERY USING THE SIMPLE QUERY WIZARD (CONTINUED)

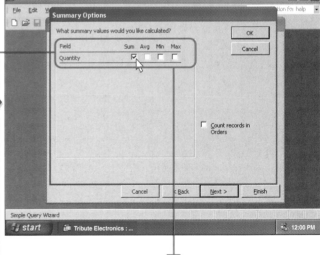

■ This screen appears if your query contains information that Access can summarize.

Note: If this screen does not appear, skip to step 16.

8 Click the way you want to display the information in the results of your query (○ changes to ⊙).

9 If you selected **Summary** in step **8**, click **Summary Options**.

*Note: If you selected **Detail** in step **8**, skip to step 15.*

■ The Summary Options dialog box appears.

■ This area displays the fields you can summarize.

10 Click the box (☐) for each calculation you want to perform (☐ changes to ☑).

Note: For information on the calculations you can perform, see the top of page 197.

**What calculations can Access perform
to summarize data in my query?**

Sum

Adds the values.

Avg

Calculates the
average value.

Min

Finds the smallest
value.

Max

Finds the largest
value.

Count records

Counts the number
of records.

‑**11** To count the number of
records used in each group to
perform the calculations, click
this option (☐ changes to ☑).

12 Click **OK** to confirm
your selections.

‑**13** Click **Next** to continue.

■ You can click **Back**
at any time to return to a
previous step and change
your selections.

CONTINUED

CREATE A QUERY USING THE SIMPLE QUERY WIZARD

If a field in your query contains dates, you can specify the way you want to group the dates in your query.

You can group dates by day, month, quarter or year.

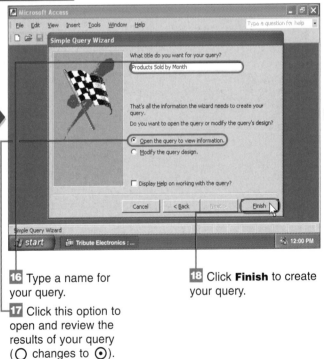

■ This screen appears if a field in your query contains dates and you chose to summarize data in your query in step 8.

14 Click the way you want to group the dates in your query (○ changes to ⊙).

15 Click **Next** to continue.

16 Type a name for your query.

17 Click this option to open and review the results of your query (○ changes to ⊙).

18 Click **Finish** to create your query.

Why didn't my query summarize data the way I expected?

To ensure that Access will properly summarize data in your query, make sure you include only the fields you need to summarize data. For example, to determine the total number of units sold by each employee, you should include only the Employee and Units Sold fields.

Employee	Units Sold
Abbott	8,800
Carey	7,400
Davis	3,900
Jones	3,700
Lance	7,700
McMillan	8,800

Can I make changes to a query I created using the Simple Query Wizard?

Yes. You can use the Design view of a query to make changes to any query you create. For example, you can sort records and add and remove fields. To display a query in the Design view, see page 200.

■ The results of your query appear.

19 When you finish reviewing the results of your query, click ☒ to close the query.

■ The query appears in the Database window.

■ To once again open the query to review the results of the query, double-click the query in the Database window.

Note: Each time you open a query, Access will use the most current data from your database to determine the results of the query.

CHANGE THE VIEW OF A QUERY

You can view a query in five different ways. Each view allows you to perform different tasks.

Design View　　Datasheet View　　SQL View

Select View

CHANGE THE VIEW OF A QUERY

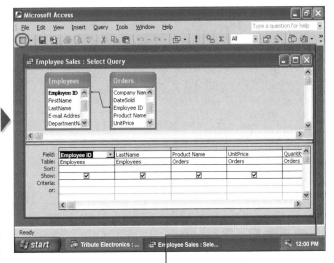

■ In this example, the query appears in the Datasheet view.

1 Click ▾ in this area to display the query in a different view.

2 Click the view you want to use.

■ The query appears in the view you selected.

■ In this example, the View button changed from ▨ to ▥.

■ To quickly switch between the Datasheet (▥) and Design (▨) views, click the View button.

200

THE QUERY VIEWS

Design View

The Design view allows you to plan your query. You can use this view to specify the data you want to find, where Access can find the data and how you want to display the results.

Datasheet View

The Datasheet view displays the results of your query. The field names appear across the top of the window. Each row shows the information for one record that meets the conditions you specified.

SQL View

The SQL view displays the SQL statements for your query. SQL (Structured Query Language) is a computer language used to work with the information in a database. When you create a query, Access creates the SQL statements that describe your query.

PivotTable View

The PivotTable view allows you to summarize and analyze the results of your query. When you first display your query results in this view, the PivotTable is empty and you must add the fields you want the PivotTable to display. For information on using the PivotTable view, see page 232.

PivotChart View

The PivotChart view allows you to display a graphical summary of the results of your query. When you first display your query results in this view, the PivotChart is empty and you must add the fields you want the PivotChart to display. For information on using the PivotChart view, see page 238.

OPEN A QUERY

You can open a query to display the results of the query on your screen. Opening a query allows you to review and make changes to the query.

Each time you open a query, Access will use the most current data from your database to determine the results of the query.

OPEN A QUERY

1 Click **Queries** in the Database window.

■ This area displays a list of the queries in your database.

2 Double-click the query you want to open.

■ The query opens, displaying the results of the query.

■ When you finish reviewing and working with the query, click ✕ to close the query.

*Note: A dialog box will appear if you did not save changes you made to the design of the query. Click **Yes** or **No** to specify if you want to save the changes.*

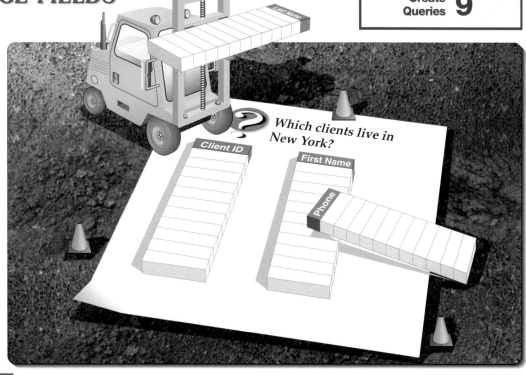

You can change the
order of fields in a
query. Rearranging
fields in a query will
affect the order in
which the fields will
appear in the query
results.

REARRANGE FIELDS

1 Display the query you
want to change in the Design
view. To change the view of
a query, see page 200.

2 Position the mouse ⌐
directly above the field you
want to move (⌐ changes
to ↓) and then click to select
the field. The field is highlighted.

3 Position the mouse ⌐
directly above the selected
field and then drag the
field to a new location.

*Note: A thick line shows where
the field will appear.*

■ The field appears
in the new location.

4 Click 🖫 to save
your change.

ADD FIELDS

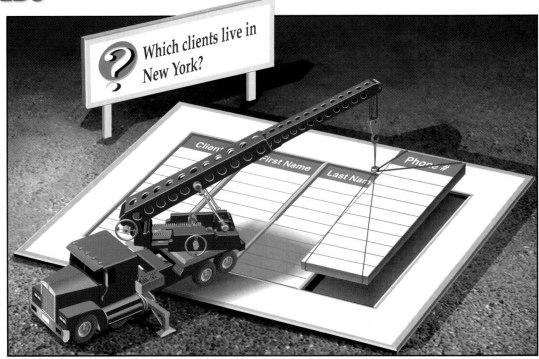

You can add one or all the fields in a table to a query. All the fields you add will appear in the results of the query.

Adding a field to a query is useful if you did not include a field from a table when you created a query.

ADD ONE FIELD

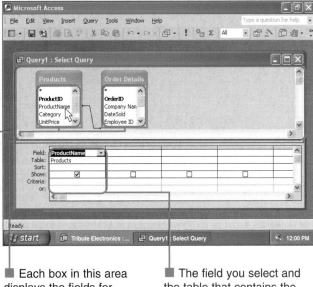

■ Each box in this area displays the fields for one table.

1 Double-click the field you want to add to your query.

■ The field you select and the table that contains the field appear in a column.

ADD ALL FIELDS

1 Double-click the heading of the box for the table that contains the fields you want to add to your query.

■ All the fields in the table are selected.

2 Position the mouse ⌖ over the selected fields and then drag the fields to the first empty column.

■ Each field from the table appears in its own column.

Why would I use the asterisk (*) to add all the fields in a table to a query?

If you may later add or delete fields from a table used in a query, you may want to use the asterisk (*) to add all the fields in the table to the query. When you add or delete a field from the table, Access will automatically add or delete the field from the query.

How can I clear a query to start over?

If you make mistakes while adding fields to a query, you can start over by clearing the query.

1 Click **Edit**.

2 Click **Clear Grid**.

Note: If Clear Grid is not displayed, position the mouse over the bottom of the menu to display the option.

ADD ALL FIELDS USING THE ASTERISK (*)

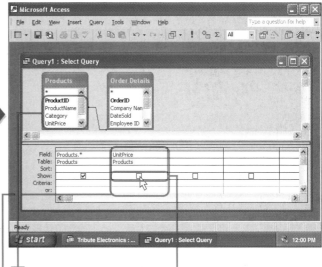

1 Double-click the asterisk (*) in the box for the table containing the fields you want to add to your query.

■ The name of the table followed by an asterisk (*) appears in a column. All the fields in the table will appear in the results of your query.

2 To set criteria or other options for one field in the table, double-click the field to place the field in a separate column.

■ The field appears in a separate column in the query.

Note: To set criteria for the field, see page 209.

3 To ensure the field will not appear twice in the query results, click the **Show** box for the field (☑ changes to ☐).

205

DELETE A FIELD

You can delete a field you no longer want to include in your query.

When you delete a field from a query, Access will not delete the field from the table you used to create the query.

1 To select the field you want to delete, position the mouse ⅛ directly above the field (⅛ changes to ↓) and then click to select the field. The field is highlighted.

2 Press the `Delete` key to delete the field.

■ The field disappears from your query.

You can hide a field used in a query. Hiding a field is useful when you need a field to find information in your database, but do not want the field to appear in the results of your query.

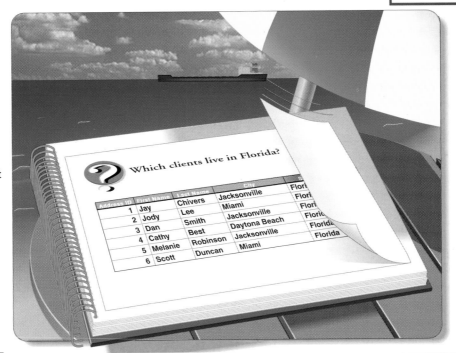

For example, you can use the State field in a query to find all your clients in Florida, but hide the State field in the query results.

HIDE A FIELD

■ Each field that displays a check mark (✔) will appear in the results of your query.

1 If you do not want a field to appear in the results of your query, click the **Show** box for the field (✔ changes to ☐).

2 Click **!** to run the query.

■ The field does not appear in the results of the query.

■ To return to the Design view, click ⬚.

■ If you no longer want to hide a field in the results of your query, repeat step 1 (☐ changes to ✔).

SORT QUERY RESULTS

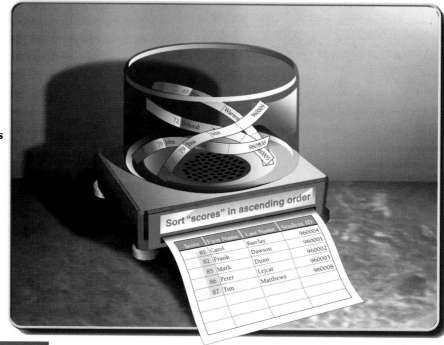

You can sort the results of a query to better organize the results. Sorting the query results can help you quickly find information of interest.

Sort "scores" in ascending order

You can sort the results of a query in two ways.

Ascending
Sorts A to Z, 1 to 9

Descending
Sorts Z to A, 9 to 1

SORT QUERY RESULTS

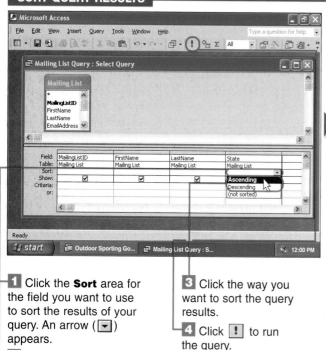

1 Click the **Sort** area for the field you want to use to sort the results of your query. An arrow (▼) appears.

2 Click the arrow (▼) to list the available sort options.

3 Click the way you want to sort the query results.

4 Click ! to run the query.

■ The records appear in the order you specified. In this example, the records are sorted alphabetically by state.

■ To return to the Design view, click ◪.

■ If you no longer want to use a field to sort the query results, repeat steps **1** to **3**, selecting **(not sorted)** in step **3**.

208

You can use criteria to find specific records in your database. Criteria are conditions that identify which records you want to find.

Which customers live in California?

State: =CA

Which students scored greater than 80% on their final grade?

Final grade: >80

Which recipes take less than 15 minutes to prepare?

Preparation Time: <15

For example, you can use criteria to find all of your customers who live in California.

USING CRITERIA TO FIND RECORDS

1 Click the **Criteria** area for the field you want to use to find specific records.

2 Type the criteria and then press the **Enter** key. Access may add quotation marks (" ") or number signs (#) to the criteria you type.

Note: For examples of criteria you can use, see page 212.

3 Click ! to run the query.

■ The results of the query appear.

■ In this example, Access found customers who ordered more than 1000 units.

■ To return to the Design view, click ⬚.

USING MULTIPLE CRITERIA TO FIND RECORDS

You can use multiple criteria to find specific records in your database.

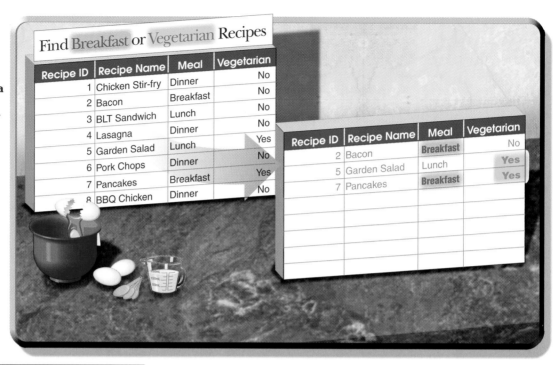

Find Breakfast or Vegetarian Recipes

Recipe ID	Recipe Name	Meal	Vegetarian
1	Chicken Stir-fry	Dinner	No
2	Bacon	Breakfast	No
3	BLT Sandwich	Lunch	No
4	Lasagna	Dinner	No
5	Garden Salad	Lunch	Yes
6	Pork Chops	Dinner	No
7	Pancakes	Breakfast	Yes
8	BBQ Chicken	Dinner	No

Recipe ID	Recipe Name	Meal	Vegetarian
2	Bacon	Breakfast	No
5	Garden Salad	Lunch	Yes
7	Pancakes	Breakfast	Yes

Criteria are conditions that identify which records you want to find. For examples of criteria that you can use, see page 212.

USING MULTIPLE CRITERIA WITH "OR"

1 Click the **Criteria** area for the first field you want to use to find specific records. Then type the first criteria.

2 Click the **or** area for the second field you want to use. Then type the second criteria.

Note: You can type the second criteria in the or area of the same field or a different field.

3 Click ![] to run the query.

■ The results of the query appear.

■ In this example, Access found customers who live in New York or Illinois.

■ To return to the Design view, click ![].

How can I use multiple criteria to find specific records in my database?

You can use the **Or** operator to find records that meet at least one of the criteria you specify. For example, you can find employees in the Sales or Accounting department.

Department
Sales
Sales
Accounting
Marketing

You can use the **And** operator to find records that meet all of the criteria you specify. For example, you can find employees in the Sales department who earn more than $60,000.

Department	Salary
Production	$57,000
Sales	$67,000
Sales	$70,000
Marketing	$65,000
Sales	$50,000

How do I use the "And" operator in one field?

In the Criteria area for the field, type the first criteria you want to use, type **And**, and then type the second criteria. For example, to find customers who purchased more than 100 units and less than 200 units, type **>100 And <200** in the Quantity field.

Field:	Quantity
Table:	Order Details
Sort:	
Show:	☑
Criteria:	>100 And <200
or:	

USING MULTIPLE CRITERIA WITH "AND"

1 Click the **Criteria** area for the first field you want to use to find specific records. Then type the first criteria.

2 Click the **Criteria** area for the second field you want to use. Then type the second criteria.

3 Click 🔘 to run the query.

■ The results of the query appear.

■ In this example, Access found customers living in New York who purchased more than 50 units.

■ To return to the Design view, click 📭.

EXAMPLES OF CRITERIA

Here are examples of criteria
that you can use to find records
in your database. Criteria are
conditions that identify which
records you want to find.

Exact matches

=100   Finds the number 100.

=California   Finds California.

=3/6/2002   Finds the date 6-Mar-02.

=Date( )   Finds today's date.

*Note: You can leave out the equal sign (=) when
searching for an exact match.*

Less than

<100   Finds numbers less
than 100.

<N   Finds text starting
with the letters A to M.

<3/6/2002   Finds dates before
6-Mar-02.

Less than or equal to

<=100   Finds numbers less
than or equal to 100.

<=N   Finds the letter N and
text starting with the
letters A to M.

<=3/6/2002   Finds dates on and
before 6-Mar-02.

Greater than

>100   Finds numbers
greater than 100.

>N   Finds text starting
with the letters N
to Z.

>3/6/2002   Finds dates after
6-Mar-02.

Greater than or equal to

>=100   Finds numbers greater
than or equal to 100.

>=N   Finds the letter N and
text starting with the
letters N to Z.

>=3/6/2002   Finds dates on and
after 6-Mar-02.

Does not match

Not 100   Finds numbers that do not match 100.

Not California   Finds text that does not match California.

Not 3/6/2002   Finds dates that do not match 6-Mar-02.

Empty fields

Is Null   Finds records that do not contain data in the field.

Is Not Null   Finds records that contain data in the field.

Find list of items

In (100,101)   Finds the numbers 100 and 101.

In (California,CA)   Finds California and CA.

In (#3/6/2002#, #3/7/2002#)   Finds the dates 6-Mar-02 and 7-Mar-02.

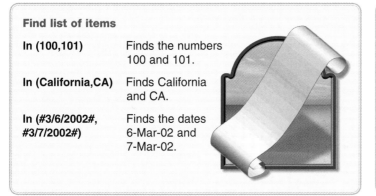

Between...And...

Between 100 And 200   Finds numbers from 100 to 200.

Between A And D   Finds the letters A and D and text starting with the letters A to C.

Between 3/6/2002 And 3/12/2002   Finds dates on and between 6-Mar-02 and 12-Mar-02.

Wildcards

The asterisk (*) wildcard represents one or more characters.
The question mark (?) wildcard represents a single character.

Like Br*   Finds text starting with **Br**, such as **Br**enda and **Br**own.

Like *ar*   Finds text containing **ar**, such as **Ar**nold and M**ar**c.

Like Wend?   Finds 5-letter words starting with **Wend**, such as **Wend**i and **Wend**y.

Like *th   Finds text ending with **th**, such as Smi**th** and Griffi**th**.

Note: You can leave out "Like" when using wildcard characters.

DISPLAY HIGHEST OR LOWEST VALUES

In the results of a query, you can have Access display only the records with the highest or lowest values in a field.

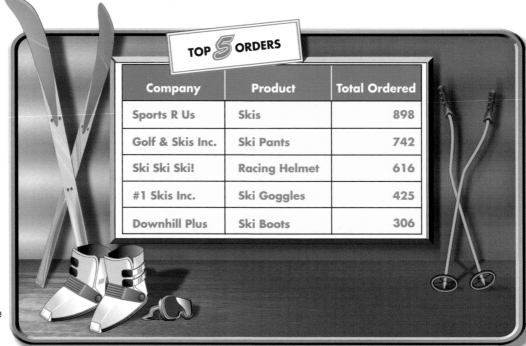

TOP 5 ORDERS

Company	Product	Total Ordered
Sports R Us	Skis	898
Golf & Skis Inc.	Ski Pants	742
Ski Ski Ski!	Racing Helmet	616
#1 Skis Inc.	Ski Goggles	425
Downhill Plus	Ski Boots	306

For example, you can display the five largest orders or the ten lowest-selling products.

DISPLAY HIGHEST OR LOWEST VALUES

1 Click the Sort area for the field you want to display the highest or lowest values for. An arrow (▼) appears.

2 Click the arrow (▼) to display a list of sort options.

3 Click the way you want to sort the records.

Ascending
Display lowest values

Descending
Display highest values

Why didn't the results of my query appear the way I expected?

If you have set up other fields to sort the results of your query, Access may not display the highest or lowest values in a field properly. To remove a sort from a field, perform steps **1** to **3** below, selecting **(not sorted)** in step **3**.

? Find Top 5 Products Sold

Product	Units Sold
Superior Race Top	4,068
Extreme Socks	3,749
Baldwin Shorts	2,562
Stay Cool Hat	2,378
Dual Purpose Shades	1,584

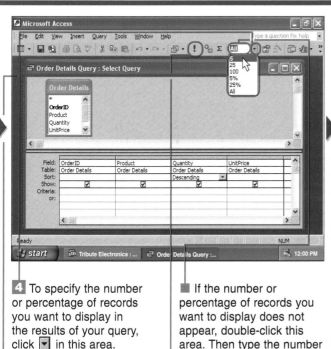

■ **4** To specify the number or percentage of records you want to display in the results of your query, click ▼ in this area.

■ **5** Click the number or percentage of records you want to display.

■ If the number or percentage of records you want to display does not appear, double-click this area. Then type the number or percentage of records you want to display.

■ **6** Click ! to run the query.

■ The number or percentage of records you specified appear in the results of your query.

■ In this example, the records with the five highest values in the field appear.

■ To return to the Design view, click.

■ To once again display all the records in the results of the query, repeat steps **4** and **5**, selecting **All** in step **5**.

You can perform a calculation on each record in a query. You can then review and analyze the results.

Job ID	Rate/Hr	Hours	Total
1	$17.00 X	8 =	$136.00
2	$25.00	11.5	$287.50
3	$20.00	18.2	$364.0
4	$30.00	4	$12
5	$60.00	27.5	

You can use these operators to perform calculations.

+ Add
- Subtract
* Multiply
/ Divide
^ Raise to a power

PERFORM CALCULATIONS

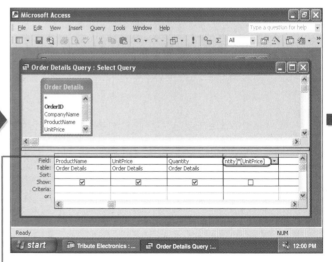

1 Click the **Field** area in the first empty column.

2 Type a name for the field that will display the results of the calculations, followed by a colon (:). Then press the **Spacebar** to leave a blank space.

3 Type an expression that describes the calculation you want to perform. In this example, type the expression **[Quantity]*[UnitPrice]**. For information on entering expressions, see the top of page 217.

Note: If the expression you type is too long to fit in the cell, you can zoom into the cell to display the contents of the entire cell. To zoom into a cell, see page 58.

How do I enter an expression to perform a calculation?

[Quantity]*[Price]

To enter fields in an expression, type the field names in square brackets. Make sure you type the field names exactly.

[Orders]![Quantity]*[Orders]![Price]

If a field exists in more than one table, you need to type the name of the table that contains the field in square brackets followed by an exclamation mark (!). Then type the field name in square brackets. Make sure you type the table and field names exactly.

Orders		
Quantity	**Price**	**Total**
100	$42	$4,200
50	$50	$2,500
70	$75	$5,250
30	$36	$1,080
90	$45	$4,050

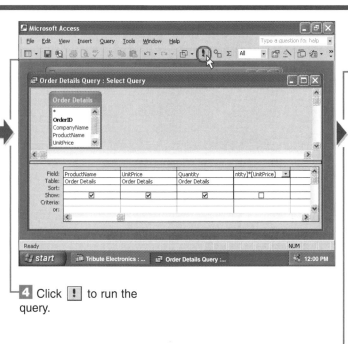

4 Click ❗ to run the query.

■ The results of the calculations appear. The field name you specified appears at the top of the column.

5 To save the changes you made to your query, click 🔘.

■ To return to the Design view, click 📝.

Note: Access does not store the results of calculations in your database. Each time you run a query, Access will use the most current data in your database to perform the calculations.

USING PARAMETERS

You can use a parameter to be able to specify the information you want to find each time you run a query.

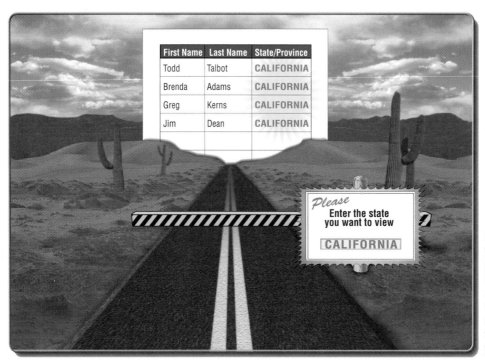

For example, you can use a parameter to have Access request the name of the state you want to find each time you run a query.

USING PARAMETERS

1 Click the **Criteria** area for the field you want to use a parameter.

2 Type an operator for the parameter.

Note: For examples of operators you can use, see the top of page 219.

3 Type the message you want Access to display when you run the query. Enclose the message in square brackets [ ].

Note: If the message you type is too long to fit in the cell, you can zoom into the cell to display the contents of the entire cell. To zoom into a cell, see page 58.

When entering a parameter, what operators can I use?

Operator	Result
=	Finds data equal to the value you enter.
>	Finds data greater than the value you enter.
>=	Finds data greater than or equal to the value you enter.
<	Finds data less than the value you enter.
<=	Finds data less than or equal to the value you enter.
<>	Finds data not equal to the value you enter.

Can I use more than one parameter?

Yes. You can enter a parameter for each field you want to use a parameter. When you run the query, Access will display the Enter Parameter Value dialog box for each parameter you entered. For example, you can enter one parameter that requests a company name and a second parameter that requests the number of orders for the company greater than a certain value.

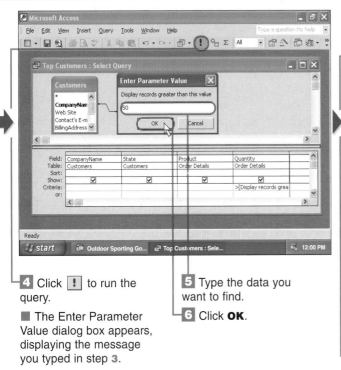

4 Click ! to run the query.

■ The Enter Parameter Value dialog box appears, displaying the message you typed in step **3**.

5 Type the data you want to find.

6 Click **OK**.

■ The results of the query appear. In this example, Access found customers who ordered more than 50 units.

7 To save the changes you made to your query, click 🖫.

■ To return to the Design view, click 🖼.

■ Each time you run the query, the Enter Parameter Value dialog box will appear, asking you to type the data you want to find.

SUMMARIZE DATA

You can summarize the data in a field to help you analyze the data.

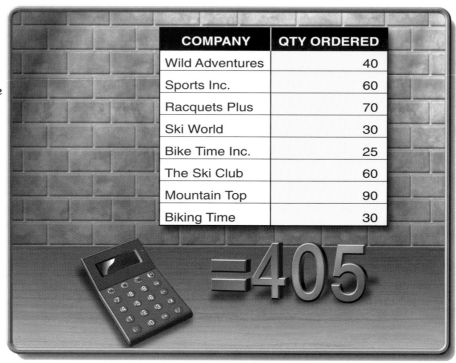

COMPANY	QTY ORDERED
Wild Adventures	40
Sports Inc.	60
Racquets Plus	70
Ski World	30
Bike Time Inc.	25
The Ski Club	60
Mountain Top	90
Biking Time	30

=405

For example, you can summarize the data in the Quantity Ordered field to determine the total number of products ordered.

SUMMARIZE DATA FOR ONE FIELD

1 Create a query that includes only the field you want to summarize. To create a query in the Design view, see page 190.

2 Click Σ to display the Total row.

■ The Total row appears.

3 Click the **Total** area for the field. An arrow (▼) appears.

4 Click the arrow (▼) to display a list of calculations that you can perform.

What calculations can I perform to summarize data?

Sum	Adds the values.
Avg	Calculates the average value.
Min	Finds the smallest value.
Max	Finds the largest value.
Count	Counts the number of values.
StDev	Calculates the standard deviation of the values.
Var	Calculates the variance of the values.
First	Finds the value of the first record entered.
Last	Finds the value of the last record entered.

Can I summarize the data for more than one field?

Yes. You can summarize the data for more than one field. For example, you can summarize the data for both the Units in Stock and Units on Order fields. When creating your query, make sure you include each field you want to summarize and specify the calculations you want to perform on the data in each field.

Product	Units in Stock	Units on Order
Hockey Gloves	25	15
Hockey Stick	125	59
Hockey Helmet	50	10
Hockey Shin Pads	21	5
Skates	45	15
Putter	33	25
Golf Driver	21	9
Golf Glove	45	23
Skis	22	10
Ski Poles	24	12
Ski Boots	35	8

=446 =191

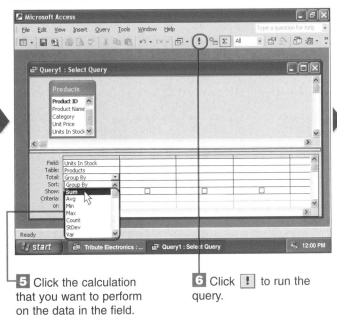

5 Click the calculation that you want to perform on the data in the field.

Note: For information on the calculations that you can perform, see the top of this page.

6 Click ❗ to run the query.

■ The result of the calculation appears.

■ In this example, Access calculates the total number of units in stock for all products.

■ To return to the Design view, click 📉.

■ If you no longer want your query to summarize the data in a field, repeat step **2** to remove the Total row from your query.

CONTINUED

SUMMARIZE DATA

You can group records in your database and summarize the data for each group.

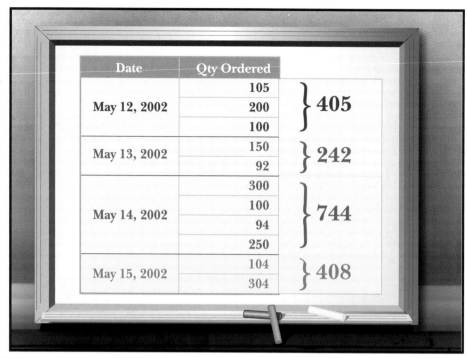

Date	Qty Ordered	
May 12, 2002	105	
	200	} 405
	100	
May 13, 2002	150	} 242
	92	
May 14, 2002	300	
	100	} 744
	94	
	250	
May 15, 2002	104	} 408
	304	

For example, you can group records by date and determine the total number of orders for each day.

SUMMARIZE DATA FOR GROUPED RECORDS

1 Create a query that includes only the field you want to use to group your records and the field you want to summarize. To create a query in the Design view, see page 190.

2 Click Σ to display the Total row.

■ The Total row appears.

3 Click the **Total** area for the field you want to summarize. An arrow (▾) appears.

4 Click the arrow (▾) to display a list of calculations that you can perform.

5 Click the calculation that you want to perform on the data in the field.

Note: For information on the calculations that you can perform, see the top of page 221.

Can I use more than one field to group records?

Yes. You can group records using more than one field. For example, to determine the total amount of each product purchased by each company, use the Company and Product fields to group records and the Quantity Ordered field to summarize data. When creating your query, make sure you place the fields in the order that you want to group the records. Access will group the records using the fields from left to right.

COMPANY	PRODUCT	QUANTITY ORDERED
Fitness Minds	A	40
Fitness Minds	B	60
Racquets Plus	A	80
Racquets Plus	B	30
Ski World	A	25
Ski World	B	60
SportStop	A	90
SportStop	B	100

■ Access will group the records using the field that displays **Group By**.

6 Click ! to run the query.

■ The results of the calculations appear.

■ In this example, Access calculates the total number of units in stock for each product.

■ To return to the Design view, click.

■ If you no longer want your query to summarize the data for grouped records, repeat step **2** to remove the Total row from your query.

FIND UNMATCHED RECORDS

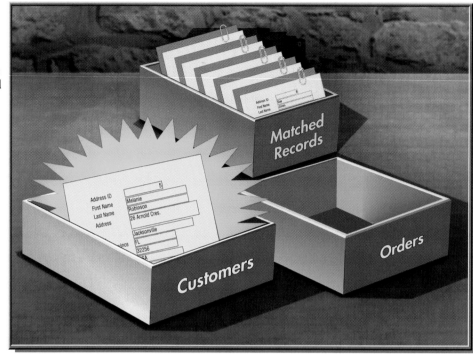

You can use the Find Unmatched Query Wizard to find records in one table that do not have matching records in another table.

For example, you can find all customers who have not placed an order.

FIND UNMATCHED RECORDS

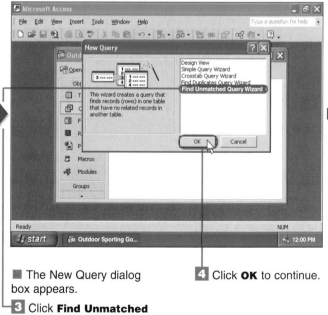

1 Click **Queries** in the Database window.

2 Click **New** to create a new query.

■ The New Query dialog box appears.

3 Click **Find Unmatched Query Wizard**.

4 Click **OK** to continue.

Why does a dialog box appear when I select the Find Unmatched Query Wizard?

When you select the Find Unmatched Query Wizard for the first time, a dialog box appears, stating that the wizard is not installed on your computer. To install the wizard, insert the CD you used to install Access into your CD drive and then click **Yes** to install the wizard.

How can I prevent unmatched records from being entered in two tables?

You can enforce referential integrity between two tables to prevent you from entering a record in one table if a matching record does not exist in a related table. For example, if a customer does not exist in the Customers table, you will not be able to enter an order for the customer in the Orders table. For more information on referential integrity, see page 128.

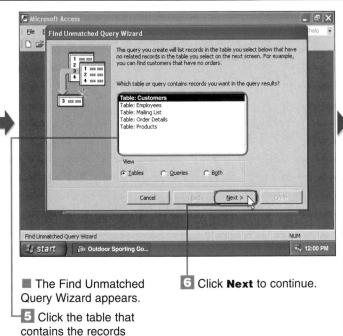

■ The Find Unmatched Query Wizard appears.

5 Click the table that contains the records you want to display in the query results if another table does not have matching records.

6 Click **Next** to continue.

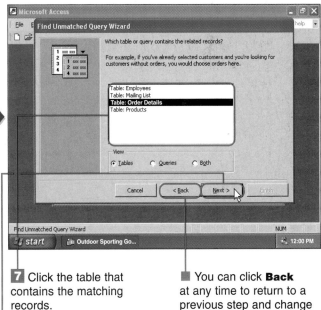

7 Click the table that contains the matching records.

8 Click **Next** to continue.

■ You can click **Back** at any time to return to a previous step and change your selections.

CONTINUED

FIND UNMATCHED RECORDS

When using the Find Unmatched Query Wizard, you need to select the field that appears in both tables so Access can compare the data in the tables.

For example, you can select the Customer ID field in the Customers and Orders tables.

FIND UNMATCHED RECORDS (CONTINUED)

9 Click the field in the first table that also appears in the second table.

10 Click the matching field in the second table.

Note: The matching fields will usually have the same name.

11 Click <=> to confirm your selections.

12 Click **Next** to continue.

■ This area displays the fields from the table you selected in step **5**.

13 Double-click each field you want to appear in the results of your query.

Note: To add all the fields in the table at once, click >> .

■ Each field you select appears in this area.

■ To remove a field you accidentally selected, double-click the field in this area.

14 Click **Next** to continue.

Do I have to recreate a query each time I want to find unmatched records in the tables?

No. Each time you open a query you created using the Find Unmatched Query Wizard, Access will use the most current data from the tables you specified to determine if any unmatched records exist in the tables.

Can I change data displayed in the results of my query?

Yes. You can change data displayed in the results of a query as you would edit data in a table. If you change the data displayed in the query results, the data will also change in the table you used to create the query. To edit data in a table, see page 56.

15 Type a name for your query.

16 Click **Finish** to display the results of your query.

■ The results of your query appear.

■ In this example, Access displays information about each customer who has not placed an order.

17 When you finish reviewing the results of your query, click ⊠ to close the query.

RENAME A QUERY

You can change the name of a query to better describe the information displayed in the query.

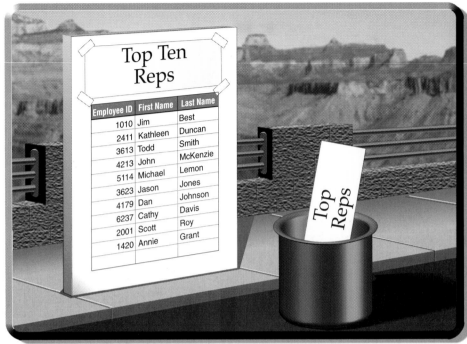

Each query in your database must have a unique name.

1 Click **Queries** in the Database window.

■ This area displays a list of the queries in your database.

2 Click the name of the query you want to rename.

3 After a few seconds, click the name of the query again or press the **F2** key. A black border appears around the name of the query.

Note: If you accidentally double-click the name of the query, the query will open.

4 Type a new name for the query and then press the **Enter** key.

■ The query displays the new name.

DELETE A QUERY

If you no longer need a query, you can permanently delete the query from your database.

DELETE A QUERY

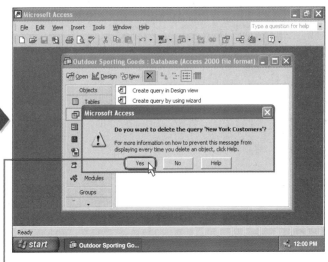

1 Click **Queries** in the Database window.

■ This area displays a list of the queries in your database.

2 Click the name of the query you want to delete.

3 Click ✕ to delete the query.

■ A confirmation dialog box appears.

4 Click **Yes** to permanently delete the query.

■ The query disappears from the Database window.

	Quarter 1 Sales	Quarter 2 Sales	Quarter 3 Sales	Grand Total
Central	$16,000.00	$19,000.00	$18,000.00	$53,000.00
North	$16,000.00	$23,000.00	$21,000.00	$60,000.00
South	$17,300.00	$19,400.00	$18,200.00	$54,900.00
Grand Total	$49,300.00	$61,400.00	$57,200.00	$167,900.00

Using the PivotTable and PivotChart Views

Are you interested in analyzing and summarizing data in your database? In this chapter, you will learn how to use the PivotTable and PivotChart views to work with your data.

USING THE PIVOTTABLE VIEW

You can use the PivotTable view to summarize and analyze the data in a table, form or the results of a query.

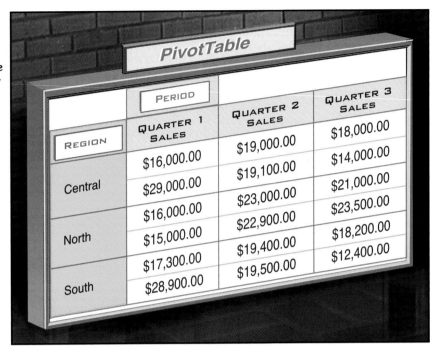

When you first display a table, form or query in the PivotTable view, the PivotTable may appear empty. You may need to add the fields you want to display to the PivotTable.

If you have previously displayed the table, form or query in the PivotChart view, the PivotTable will display the fields you added to the PivotChart. For information on the PivotChart view, see page 238.

USING THE PIVOTTABLE VIEW

1 To show the displayed table, form or query in the PivotTable view, click ▾ in this area.

2 Click **PivotTable View**.

■ The table, form or query appears in the PivotTable view.

■ The PivotTable Field List dialog box also appears, displaying the name of each field in your table, form or query.

■ If the PivotTable Field List dialog box does not appear, click 🔳 to display the dialog box.

What fields do I need to add to create a PivotTable?

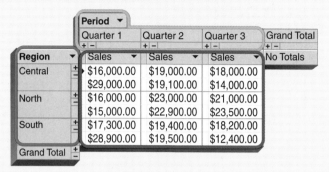

Period ▾			
Quarter 1	Quarter 2	Quarter 3	Grand Total
+ −	+ −	+ −	+ −

Region ▾	Sales ▾	Sales ▾	Sales ▾	No Totals
Central	$16,000.00	$19,000.00	$18,000.00	
	$29,000.00	$19,100.00	$14,000.00	
North	$16,000.00	$23,000.00	$21,000.00	
	$15,000.00	$22,900.00	$23,500.00	
South	$17,300.00	$19,400.00	$18,200.00	
	$28,900.00	$19,500.00	$12,400.00	
Grand Total				

Totals or Detail Field

Specifies a field that contains the data you want to summarize in the table.

Row Field

Specifies a field you want to use to group data in the table. The name of each group in the field appears down the left side of the table.

Column Field

Specifies a field you want to use to group data in the table. The name of each group in the field appears across the top of the table.

3 To add a field that contains the data you want to summarize in the table, position the mouse ◻ over the name of the field in this area.

4 Drag the field name to the **Drop Totals or Detail Fields Here** area.

■ The name of the field you selected appears in this area.

■ This area displays the data for each record in your table, form or query.

CONTINUED ➤

USING THE PIVOTTABLE VIEW

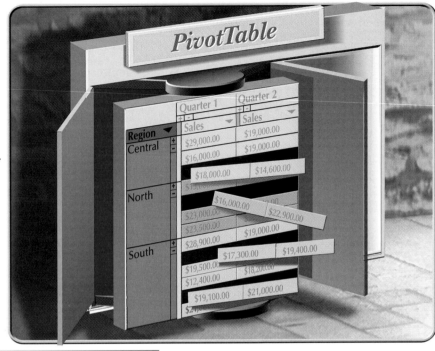

When using the PivotTable view, you can select the fields you want to use to group the data in the PivotTable.

For example, you can use the Region field to group the data by region in the PivotTable.

USING THE PIVOTTABLE VIEW (CONTINUED)

5 To add the field you want to use to group the data in the table, position the mouse �井 over the name of the field in this area.

6 Drag the field name to the **Drop Row Fields Here** area.

■ The name of the field you selected appears in this area. The name of each group in the field appears down the left side of the table.

7 To add another field you want to use to group the data in the table, position the mouse �井 over the name of the field in this area.

8 Drag the field name to the **Drop Column Fields Here** area.

Can I remove a field from a PivotTable?

Yes. You can remove any field you added to a PivotTable. Removing a field from a PivotTable will not remove the field from the table, form or query used to create the PivotTable. To remove a field from a PivotTable, click the name of the field in the PivotTable and then press the Delete key.

How can I move the PivotTable Field List dialog box so it does not cover my PivotTable?

To move the PivotTable Field List dialog box, position the mouse ℝ over the title bar of the dialog box and then drag the dialog box to a new location.

■ The name of the field you selected appears in this area. The name of each group in the field appears along the top of the table.

■ The name of each field you added to the table appears in **bold** in the PivotTable Field List dialog box.

■ Each group of data displays a plus sign (+) and a minus sign (−).

■ To hide the data in a group, click a minus sign (−).

Note: To once again display the data in a group, click a plus sign (+).

9 To save all the changes you made in the PivotTable view, click 🖫.

Note: Access automatically saves changes you make to a form displayed in the PivotTable view.

CONTINUED

You can perform calculations on the data displayed in a PivotTable to help you analyze the data.

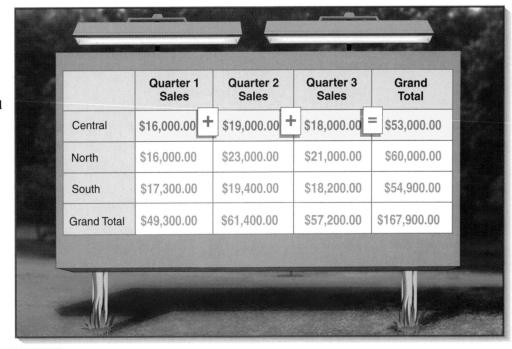

	Quarter 1 Sales	Quarter 2 Sales	Quarter 3 Sales	Grand Total
Central	$16,000.00 $+$	$19,000.00 $+$	$18,000.00 $=$	$53,000.00
North	$16,000.00	$23,000.00	$21,000.00	$60,000.00
South	$17,300.00	$19,400.00	$18,200.00	$54,900.00
Grand Total	$49,300.00	$61,400.00	$57,200.00	$167,900.00

PERFORM CALCULATIONS

1 Click the name of the field in the table that contains the data you want to perform calculations on.

■ The data in the field is highlighted.

2 Click Σ to display a list of the calculations that you can perform.

3 Click the calculation you want to perform.

Note: For information on the calculations that you can perform, see the top of page 237.

What calculations can I perform on the data in a PivotTable?

Calculation	Result
Sum	Adds the values.
Count	Counts the number of values.
Min	Finds the smallest value.
Max	Finds the largest value.
Average	Calculates the average value.
Standard Deviation	Calculates the standard deviation of the values.
Variance	Calculates the variance of the values.
Standard Deviation Population	Calculates the population standard deviation of the values.
Variance Population	Calculates the population variance of the values.

■ The table displays the subtotals and grand totals for the calculation you selected.

■ The name of the new total field appears at the top of the PivotTable Field List dialog box.

4 To save the change you made in the PivotTable view, click ![save].

Note: Access automatically saves changes you make to a form displayed in the PivotTable view.

REMOVE CALCULATIONS

1 To remove calculations from a table, right-click the name of the total field in the PivotTable Field List dialog box. A menu appears.

■ If the PivotTable Field List dialog box does not appear, click ![icon] to display the dialog box.

2 Click **Delete**.

■ The field will disappear from the PivotTable Field List dialog box and the calculations will disappear from the table.

USING THE PIVOTCHART VIEW

You can use the PivotChart view to display a graphical summary of the data in a table, form or the results of a query.

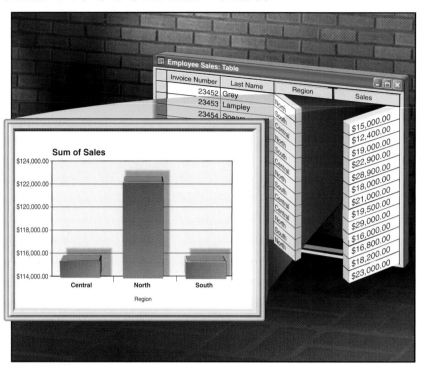

When you first display a table, form or query in the PivotChart view, the PivotChart may appear empty. You may need to add the fields you want to display to the PivotChart.

If you have previously displayed the table, form or query in the PivotTable view, the PivotChart will display the fields you added to the PivotTable. For information on the PivotTable view, see page 232.

USING THE PIVOTCHART VIEW

1 To show the displayed table, form or query in the PivotChart view, click in this area.

2 Click **PivotChart View**.

■ The table, form or query appears in the PivotChart view.

■ The Chart Field List dialog box also appears, displaying the name of each field in your table, form or query.

■ If the Chart Field List dialog box does not appear, click ▤ to display the dialog box.

What fields do I need to add to create a PivotChart?

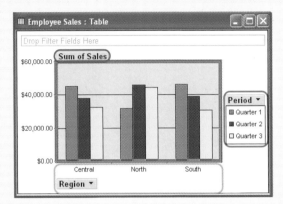

Category Field

Specifies a field you want to use to group data in the chart. The name of each group in the field appears along the bottom of the chart.

Series Field

Specifies a field that contains the data you want to display as separate data series in the chart. Each data series is represented by a specific color, which is identified in the legend.

Data Field

Specifies a field that contains the data you want to summarize in the chart. Access will plot the summary of the data in the chart.

3 To add the field you want to use to group data in the chart, position the mouse ⬚ over the name of the field in this area.

4 Drag the field name to the **Drop Category Fields Here** area.

■ The name of the field you selected appears in this area.

■ The name of each group in the field appears along the bottom of the chart.

Note: The name of each group in the field may not appear in the chart until after you perform step 6.

CONTINUED

USING THE PIVOTCHART VIEW

When using the PivotChart view, you can select the field that contains the data you want to summarize in the PivotChart.

Access will plot the summary of the data in the PivotChart. For example, Access will display the total sales for each region.

5 To add the field that contains the data you want to summarize in the chart, position the mouse ⊾ over the name of the field in this area.

6 Drag the field name to the **Drop Data Fields Here** area.

■ The name of the field you selected appears in this area.

■ Access summarizes the data for each group in the chart.

7 To add a field that contains the data you want to display as separate data series in the chart, position the mouse ⊾ over the name of the field in this area.

8 Drag the field name to the **Drop Series Fields Here** area.

Can I remove a field from a PivotChart?

Yes. You can remove any field you added to a PivotChart. Removing a field from a PivotChart will not remove the field from the table, form or query used to create the PivotChart. To remove a field from a PivotChart, click the name of the field in the PivotChart and then press the Delete key.

How can I move the Chart Field List dialog box so it does not cover my PivotChart?

To move the Chart Field List dialog box, position the mouse ⌖ over the title bar of the dialog box and then drag the dialog box to a new location.

■ The name of the field you selected appears in this area.

■ Access displays a data series for each group of data in the field.

9 To display a legend that identifies the color used for each data series in the chart, click 📧.

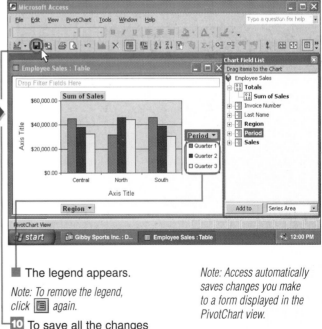

■ The legend appears.

Note: To remove the legend, click 📧 again.

10 To save all the changes you made in the PivotChart view, click 💾.

Note: Access automatically saves changes you make to a form displayed in the PivotChart view.

CONTINUED

241

USING THE PIVOTCHART VIEW

You can change the chart type of a PivotChart to present your data more effectively.

CHANGE THE CHART TYPE

1 Click a blank area in the chart you want to change to a different chart type.

2 Click to change the chart type.

■ The Properties dialog box appears.

3 Click the type of chart you want to use.

■ This area displays the available chart designs for the type of chart you selected.

4 Click the chart design you want to use.

■ Access changes the chart type of the chart.

5 Click ☒ to close the Properties dialog box.

You can change the type of calculation that Access performs on the data in a PivotChart to help you better analyze the data.

Sum of Sales

Average of Sales

For example, Access can calculate the average value for each group in a PivotChart.

CHANGE THE CALCULATION PERFORMED

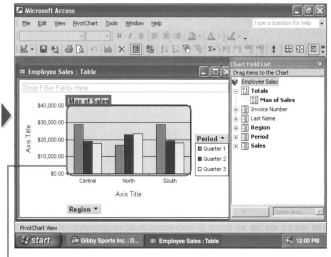

1 Click the name of the field in the chart that contains the data that Access has summarized in the chart.

2 Click Σ to display a list of the calculations that you can perform.

3 Click the calculation you want to perform.

Note: For information on the calculations that you can perform, see the top of page 237.

■ The chart shows the results of the calculation you specified.

243

Orders

ID	Payment Date	Company Name	Payment Amount	Order Number
1	2/15/02	Big League Inc.	$125.00	90384
2	2/11/02	Ski World	$400.00	12397
3	2/2/02	Varsity Supply	$299.99	10933
			$200.00	90121
	2/20		$300.00	19011
6	2/17/01	The Sport Suppliers	$575.00	23896
7	2/11/02	Athlete's Corner	$210.00	21893
8	2/16/02	Recreation Inc.	$500.00	23954

Tuesday, February 26, 2002

Create Reports

Would you like Access to help you present your data in a neatly organized report? This chapter teaches you how to create and work with reports.

CREATE A REPORT USING THE REPORT WIZARD

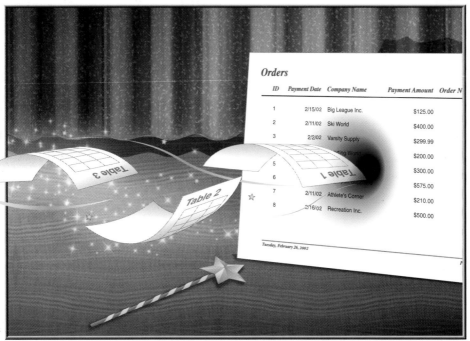

You can use the Report Wizard to create a professionally designed report that summarizes data in your database.

The Report Wizard asks you a series of questions and then creates a report based on your answers.

CREATE A REPORT USING THE REPORT WIZARD

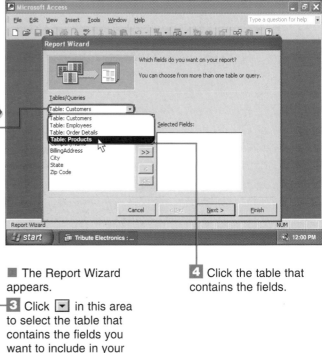

1 Click **Reports** in the Database window.

2 Double-click **Create report by using wizard**.

■ The Report Wizard appears.

3 Click ⬇ in this area to select the table that contains the fields you want to include in your report.

4 Click the table that contains the fields.

Which tables in my database can I use to create a report?

You can use any table in your database to create a report. When creating a report that uses information from more than one table, relationships must exist between the tables so that Access can bring together the information in the tables. For information on relationships, see page 124.

Can I create a report using data from a query?

Yes. When creating a report, you can use data from queries. The Report Wizard allows you to select the fields you want to include from queries as you would select the fields you want to include from tables. For information on queries, see pages 190 to 229.

■ This area displays the fields from the table you selected.

5 Double-click each field you want to include in your report.

Note: To add all the fields in the table at once, click `>>` .

■ Each field you select appears in this area.

■ To remove a field you accidentally selected, double-click the field in this area.

Note: To remove all the fields at once, click `<<` .

6 To include fields from other tables in your database, repeat steps **3** to **5** for each table.

7 Click **Next** to continue.

CONTINUED ▶

You can choose
how you want
to group data
in your report.
Grouping data
helps you
organize and
summarize the
data in your
report.

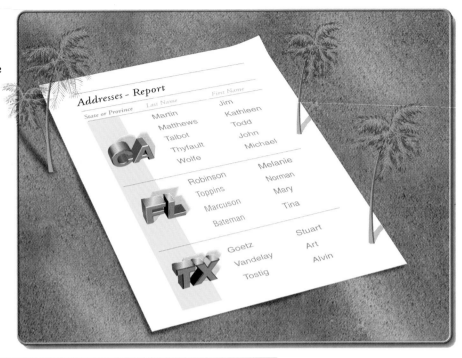

For example, you
can group data
by the State field
to place all the
customers from
the same state
together in your
report.

CREATE A REPORT USING THE REPORT WIZARD (CONTINUED)

■ If you selected fields
from more than one table,
you can choose the way
you want to group the
data in your report.

*Note: If this screen does not
appear, skip to step 10.*

8 Click the way you
want to group the data
in your report.

■ This area shows how
Access will group the
data in your report.

9 Click **Next** to continue.

10 To use a specific field
to group data in your report,
double-click the field you
want to use.

■ This area shows how
Access will group the data
in your report. The field you
selected appears in blue.

■ To remove a field you
accidentally selected to
group data in your report,
double-click the field in
this area.

11 Click **Next** to continue.

Why would I sort the records in my report?

You can sort the records in your report to better organize the data. For example, you can sort records alphabetically by the Last Name field to make it easier to find customers of interest. If the same last name appears more than once in the field, you can sort records by a second field, such as First Name, to further organize the data. You can use up to four fields to sort the records in a report.

12 To sort the records in your report, click ▾ in this area.

Note: For information on sorting, see the top of this page.

13 Click the field you want to use to sort the records.

14 Click this button until the button displays the way you want to sort the records.

Ascending–Sorts A to Z, 1 to 9

Descending–Sorts Z to A, 9 to 1

15 To sort by a second field, repeat steps **12** to **14** in this area.

CONTINUED ▶

CREATE A REPORT USING THE REPORT WIZARD

You can perform calculations to summarize the data in your report.

Sum
Add the values.

Avg
Calculate the average value.

Min
Find the smallest value.

Max
Find the largest value.

CREATE A REPORT USING THE REPORT WIZARD (CONTINUED)

16 To perform calculations in your report, click **Summary Options**.

Note: If you chose not to group data in your report, Summary Options will not be available. If Summary Options is not available, skip to step 21.

■ The Summary Options dialog box appears.

■ This area displays the fields you can perform calculations on.

17 Click the box (☐) for each calculation you want to perform (☐ changes to ☑).

18 Click an option to specify if you want the report to display all the records and the summary information or just the summary (○ changes to ⦿). For more information, see the top of page 251.

When performing calculations in my report, what information can I display?

Detail and Summary

Display all the records and the summary information. For example, show all the orders and the total orders for each month.

Summary Only

Display only the summary information. For example, show only the total orders for each month.

Calculate percent of total for sums

Display the percentage of the total that each group represents. For example, show the percentage of the total orders that each month represents.

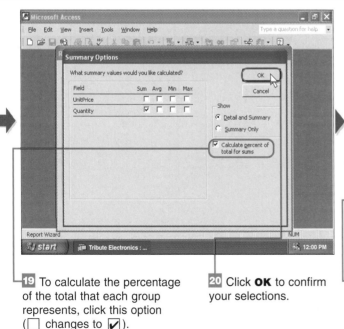

19 To calculate the percentage of the total that each group represents, click this option (☐ changes to ☑).

20 Click **OK** to confirm your selections.

21 Click **Next** to continue.

■ You can click **Back** at any time to return to a previous step and change your selections.

CONTINUED

CREATE A REPORT USING THE REPORT WIZARD

You can choose from several layouts for your report. The layout you choose determines the arrangement of information in your report.

22 Click the layout you want to use for your report (○ changes to ●).

Note: The available layouts depend on the options you selected for your report.

■ This area displays a sample of the layout you selected.

23 Click the page orientation you want to use for your report (○ changes to ●).

24 Click **Next** to continue.

25 Click the style you want to use for your report.

■ This area displays a sample of the style you selected.

26 Click **Next** to continue.

Which page orientation should I use for my report?

The portrait orientation is the standard orientation and prints data across the short side of a page. The landscape orientation prints data across the long side of a page and can be useful when a report contains many fields.

Portrait   **Landscape**

Do I need to create a new report each time I change the data in my database?

No. Each time you open a report, Access will automatically gather the most current data from your database to create the report. This ensures that the report will always display the most up-to-date information. Access will also update the date displayed in the report. To open a report, see page 256.

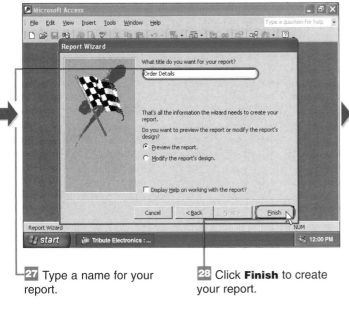

27 Type a name for your report.

28 Click **Finish** to create your report.

■ A window appears, displaying your report.

Note: To move through the pages in a report, see page 257.

29 When you finish reviewing your report, click ✕ to close the report.

CREATE A REPORT USING AN AUTOREPORT

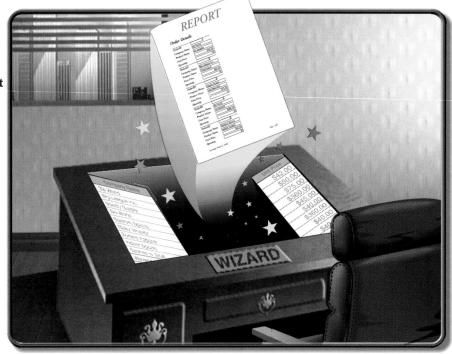

You can use the AutoReport Wizard to quickly create a report that displays the information from one table in your database.

A report summarizes the data from your database in a professional-looking document.

CREATE A REPORT USING AN AUTOREPORT

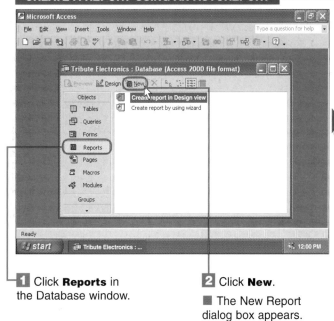

1 Click **Reports** in the Database window.

2 Click **New**.

■ The New Report dialog box appears.

3 Click the type of AutoReport you want to create.

4 Click ▼ in this area to select the table that contains the data you want to include in your report.

5 Click the table that contains the data.

6 Click **OK** to create your report.

What types of AutoReports can I create?

Columnar AutoReport

Displays the field names down the left side of each page.

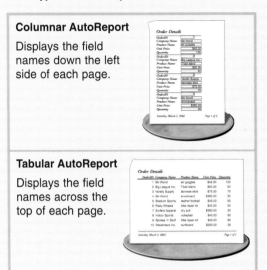

Tabular AutoReport

Displays the field names across the top of each page.

Can I change the data displayed in a report?

If you want to make changes to the data displayed in a report, you must change the data in the table you used to create the report. Changes you make to data in the table will automatically appear in the report the next time you open the report.

■ A window appears, displaying your report.

Note: To move through the pages in a report, see page 257.

7 To save your report, click **File**.

8 Click **Save**.

■ The Save As dialog box appears.

9 Type a name for your report and then press the **Enter** key.

10 When you finish reviewing your report, click ☒ to close the report.

You can open a
report to display
the contents
of the report
on your screen.
Opening a report
allows you to
review and make
changes to the
report.

Each time you
open a report,
Access uses
the most current
data from your
database to
create the report.

OPEN A REPORT

■1 Click **Reports** in the
Database window.

■ This area displays a
list of the reports in your
database.

■2 Double-click the
report you want to open.

■ The report appears. You
can now review and make
changes to the report.

■ When you finish reviewing
the report, click ✕ to close
the report.

*Note: A dialog box will appear
if you did not save changes you
made to the design of the report.
Click **Yes** or **No** to specify if you
want to save the changes.*

If your report contains more than one page, you can move through the pages to review all the information in the report.

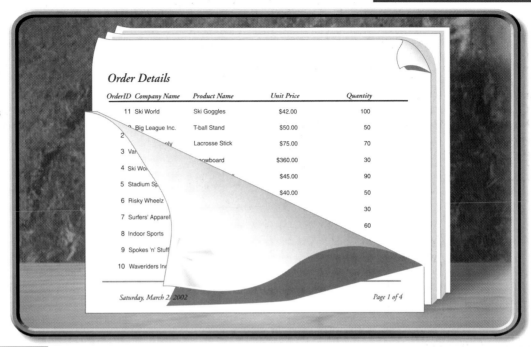

MOVE THROUGH PAGES

■ This area displays the number of the page displayed on your screen.

1 If your report contains more than one page, click one of the following buttons to display another page.

|◀◀| First page

|◀| Previous page

|▶| Next page

|▶▶| Last page

Note: If a button is dimmed, you cannot currently display that page.

MOVE TO A SPECIFIC PAGE

1 To quickly move to a specific page in your report, double-click the current page number. The page number is highlighted.

2 Type the number of the page you want to display and then press the Enter key.

CHANGE THE VIEW OF A REPORT

You can view a report in three different ways. Each view allows you to perform different tasks.

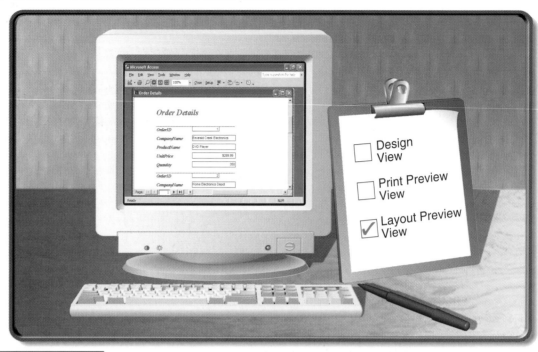

☐ Design View

☐ Print Preview View

☑ Layout Preview View

CHANGE THE VIEW OF A REPORT

■ In this example, the report appears in the Print Preview view.

1 Click ⏷ in this area to display the report in another view.

Note: The available views depend on the view you are currently using.

2 Click the view you want to use.

Note: If the view you want to use does not appear on the menu, position the mouse over the bottom of the menu to display all the views.

■ The report appears in the view you selected.

■ In this example, the View button changed from ⬚ to ⬚.

■ To quickly switch between the Print Preview (⬚) and Design (⬚) views, click the View button.

THE REPORT VIEWS

Design View

The Design view allows you to change the layout and design of a report. This view displays a grid of small, evenly spaced dots to help you line up the items in a report. Information in this view appears in several sections, such as the Report Header and Page Footer sections.

Print Preview View

The Print Preview view allows you to see how a report will look when printed. You can use this view to move through the pages in a report and examine how each page will print.

Layout Preview View

The Layout Preview view allows you to quickly view the layout and style of a report. This view is similar to the Print Preview view, but allows you to see only a few records in a report.

ZOOM IN OR OUT

When viewing a report, you can magnify an area of a page to view the area in more detail. You can also display an entire page in a report to view the overall appearance of the page.

ZOOM IN OR OUT

1 To magnify an area of a page in your report, position the mouse over the area you want to magnify (changes to).

2 Click the area to magnify the area.

■ The area appears magnified.

■ To once again display the entire page, click anywhere on the page.

■ To display two pages in your report at a time, click ⊞.

Note: To once again display only one page in your report at a time, click ▣.

You can apply an autoformat to a report to quickly change the overall appearance of the report.

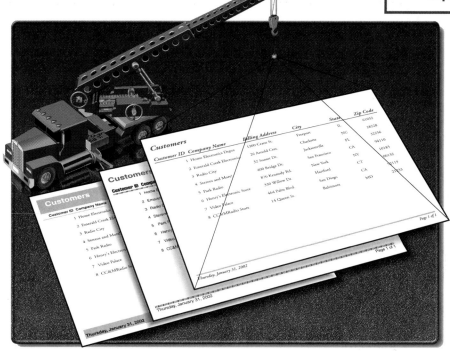

You may want to use the same autoformat for every report in your database to give your reports a consistent appearance.

APPLY AN AUTOFORMAT

1 Display the report you want to change in the Design view. To change the view of a report, see page 258.

2 Click ☐ to select the entire report (☐ changes to ☒).

3 Click ☑ to select an autoformat for the report.

■ The AutoFormat dialog box appears.

4 Click the autoformat you want to use.

■ This area displays a sample of the autoformat you selected.

5 Click **OK** to confirm your change.

■ The report will display the new autoformat.

ADD A PICTURE

You can add
a picture to
a report to
enhance the
appearance
of the report.

You can add a
picture to a report,
such as a picture
of your products
or your company
logo.

You can use a
drawing program
to create your own
picture or use a
scanner to scan an
existing picture into
your computer. You
can also buy pictures
at computer stores
or obtain pictures
on the Internet.

ADD A PICTURE

1 Display the report
you want to add a
picture to in the Design
view. To change the
view of a report, see
page 258.

2 Click 🖾 on the
Toolbox toolbar to add
a picture to your report.

■ If the Toolbox toolbar
is not displayed, click 🛠
to display the toolbar.

3 Click the location in
your report where you
want the top left corner
of the picture to appear.

■ The Insert Picture
dialog box appears.

What section of a report can I add a picture to?

You can add a picture to any section of a report. In most cases, you will want to add a picture to the Report Header section, which will display the picture at the top of the report.

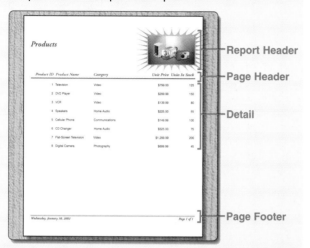

- Report Header
- Page Header
- Detail
- Page Footer

How can I delete a picture I added to a report?

To delete a picture you no longer want to appear in a report, click the picture and then press the Delete key. Access will remove the picture from the report, but will not remove the original picture from your computer.

■ This area shows the location of the displayed pictures. You can click this area to change the location.

4 Click the name of the picture you want to add to your report.

5 Click **OK** to add the picture to your report.

■ The picture appears in your report.

6 Click 🖫 to save the change you made to your report.

Note: You can move or resize a picture in a report as you would move or resize a control on a form. To move or resize a control on a form, see page 152.

RENAME A REPORT

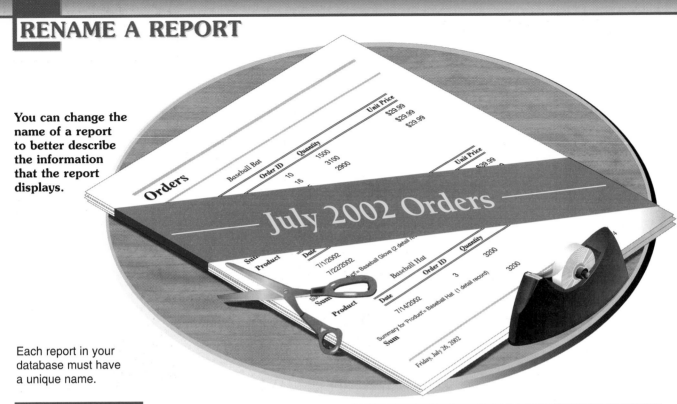

You can change the name of a report to better describe the information that the report displays.

Each report in your database must have a unique name.

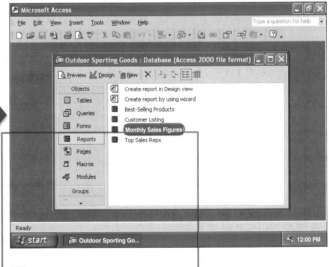

1 Click **Reports** in the Database window.

■ This area displays a list of the reports in your database.

2 Click the name of the report you want to rename.

3 After a few seconds, click the name of the report again or press the **F2** key. A black border appears around the name of the report.

Note: If you accidentally double-click the name of the report, the report will open.

4 Type a new name for the report and then press the **Enter** key.

■ The report displays the new name.

264

If you no
longer need a
report, you can
permanently
delete the
report from
your database.

DELETE A REPORT

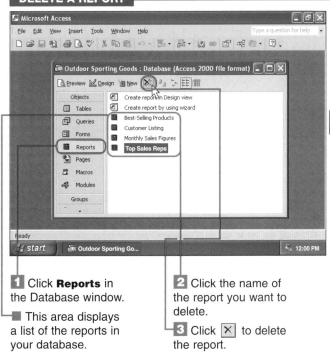

1 Click **Reports** in
the Database window.

■ This area displays
a list of the reports in
your database.

2 Click the name of
the report you want to
delete.

3 Click ☒ to delete
the report.

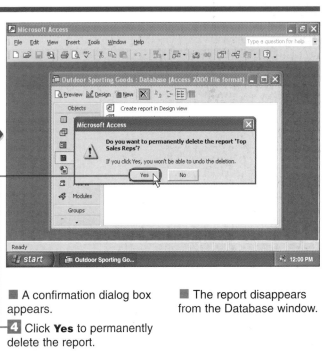

■ A confirmation dialog box
appears.

4 Click **Yes** to permanently
delete the report.

■ The report disappears
from the Database window.

Recipe ID	Recipe Name	Meal	Vegetarian
1	Chicken Stir-fry	Dinner	No
2	Omelet	Breakfast	Yes
3	Veggie Pizza	Lunch	Yes
4	Lasagna	Dinner	No
5	Pancakes	Breakfast	Yes
6	Pork Chops	Dinner	No
7	Garden Salad	Lunch	Yes
8	Fruit Salad	Breakfast	Yes

Recipe ID	Recipe Name	Meal	Vegetarian
1	Chicken Stir-fry	Dinner	No
2	Omelet	Breakfast	Yes
3	Veggie Pizza	Lunch	Yes
4	Lasagna	Dinner	No
5	Pancakes	Breakfast	Yes
6	Pork Chops	Dinner	No
7	Garden Salad	Lunch	Yes
8	Fruit Salad	Breakfast	Yes

chmitt
Linton Ave.
York, NY 10010

50 W...
Boston, MA 02117

258 Linton Ave.
New York, NY 10010

Boston, MA...

Melanie Robinson
26 Arnold Cres.
Jacksonville, FL 32...

Talbot
racker Ave.
rancisco, CA 94110

Chuck Deane
47 Crosley Ave.
Las Vegas, NV 89116

Todd Talbot
68 Cracker Ave.
San Francisco, CA 94110

Chuck Deane
47 Crosley Ave.
Las Vegas, NV 89116

Allen Toppins
10 Heldon St.
Atlanta, GA 30375

nie Robinson
rnold Cres.
sonville, FL 32256

Susan Hughes
401 Idon Dr.
Nashville, TN 37243

Melanie Robinson
26 Arnold Cres.
Jacksonville, FL 32256

Susan Hughes
401 Idon Dr.
Nashville, TN 37243

Jason Marcuson
15 Bizzo Pl.
New York, NY 1002...

Toppins
eldon St.
ta, GA 30375

Greg Kilkenny
36 Buzzard St.
Boston, MA 02118

Allen Toppins
10 Heldon St.
Atlanta, GA 30375

Greg Kilkenny
36 Buzzard St.
Boston, MA 02118

Kathleen Matthews
18 Goulage Ave.
Los Angeles, CA 900...

n Marcuson
zzo Pl.
York, NY 10020

Jim Martin
890 Apple St.
San Diego, CA 92121

Jason Marcuson
15 Bizzo Pl.
New York, NY 10020

Jim Martin
890 Apple St.
San Diego, CA 92121

een Matthews
oulage Ave.
ngeles, CA 90032

Ron Ratoff
11 Lent Ave.
Atlanta, GA 30367

Kathleen Matthews
18 Goulage Ave.
Los A...   0032

Ron Ratoff
11 Lent Ave.
Atlanta, GA 30368

SHIP TO:

Fragile
P & T Fruit Market
892 Apple St.
San Diego, CA
92121

Print Information

Are you ready to print the information in your database? In this chapter, you will learn how to preview your data before printing, change the way the data will appear on a printed page and create mailing labels.

PREVIEW BEFORE PRINTING

You can use the Print Preview feature to see how a table, query, form or report will look when printed.

The Print Preview feature can help you confirm that your printed pages will appear the way you want.

PREVIEW BEFORE PRINTING

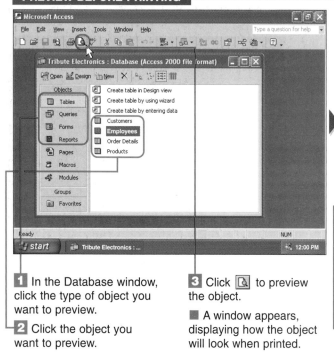

1 In the Database window, click the type of object you want to preview.

2 Click the object you want to preview.

3 Click 🔍 to preview the object.

■ A window appears, displaying how the object will look when printed.

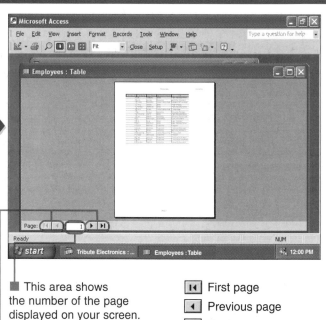

■ This area shows the number of the page displayed on your screen.

4 If the object contains more than one page, click one of the following buttons to display another page.

⏮	First page
◀	Previous page
▶	Next page
⏭	Last page

Note: If a button is dimmed, you cannot currently display that page.

268

How can I display two pages at once while previewing an object?

To display two pages at once, click the Two Pages button ( ). To once again display only one page at a time, click the One Page button ( ).

Can I see how an object will print in different views?

Yes. To see how an object will print in a specific view, display the object in the view of interest and then click the Print Preview button ( ). For example, you can display a table in the Datasheet, PivotTable or PivotChart view. To change the view of an object, see pages 74, 150, 200 and 258.

Datasheet   PivotTable   PivotChart

MAGNIFY AN AREA OF A PAGE

1 To magnify an area of a page, position the mouse over the area you want to magnify (changes to).

2 Click the area to magnify the area.

■ A magnified view of the area appears.

■ To once again display the entire page, click anywhere on the page.

CLOSE PRINT PREVIEW

1 When you finish previewing the object, click **Close** to close the preview window.

CHANGE PAGE SETUP

You can change the way information appears on a printed page.

Access stores the page setup options you specify for forms and reports so you need to specify the options only once for each form or report. For tables and queries, you must specify the page setup options every time you want to print a table or query.

CHANGE PAGE SETUP

1 In the Database window, click the type of object you want to use different page setup options.

2 Double-click the object you want to use different page setup options.

■ The object opens and appears on your screen.

3 Click **File**.

4 Click **Page Setup**.

■ The Page Setup dialog box appears.

What page setup options can I change?

Margins	**Print Headings**	**Print Data Only**	**Orientation**	**Paper Size and Source**
Determines the amount of space between data and the edges of each page.	Prints headings, which include the title, date and page numbers. This option is only available for tables and queries.	Prints only the data. This option is only available for forms and reports.	Determines which direction information prints on each page.	Specifies the paper size and the location of the paper that you want to use in the printer.

■ This area displays the margins for each page.

5 To change a margin, double-click the box beside the margin and then type a new margin.

6 If you do not want to print the title, date and page numbers, click **Print Headings** (☑ changes to ☐).

*Note: For forms and reports, the **Print Data Only** option appears instead. To print only the data in the form or report, click the option (☐ changes to ☑).*

7 Click the **Page** tab.

8 Click the page orientation you want to use (○ changes to ◉).

9 These areas display the paper size and source. You can click an area to change the paper size or source.

10 Click **OK** to confirm your changes.

Note: You can use the Print Preview feature to see how the printed pages will appear. To use the Print Preview feature, see page 268.

PRINT INFORMATION

You can produce a paper copy of a table, query, form or report.

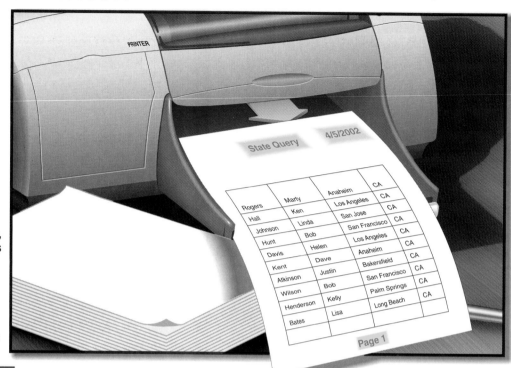

When you print a table, query or report, Access prints the title, date and page number on each page.

Before printing, make sure your printer is turned on and contains paper.

PRINT INFORMATION

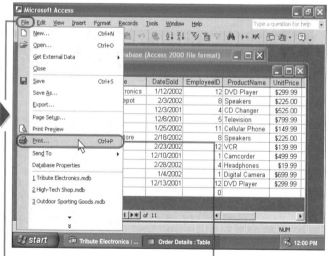

1 In the Database window, click the type of object you want to print.

2 Double-click the object you want to print.

■ The object opens and appears on your screen.

■ If you want to print only one record or a few records, select the record(s) you want to print. To select records, see page 54.

3 Click **File**.

4 Click **Print**.

■ The Print dialog box appears.

What print options can I use?

All

Prints every page.

Pages

Prints the pages you specify.

Selected Record(s)

Prints the record(s) you selected.

Can I print an object in a different view?

Yes. Before you print an object, make sure you display the object in the view you want to print the object. For example, you can display a table in the Datasheet, PivotTable or PivotChart view. To change the view of an object, see pages 74, 150, 200 and 258.

Datasheet   **PivotTable**   **PivotChart**

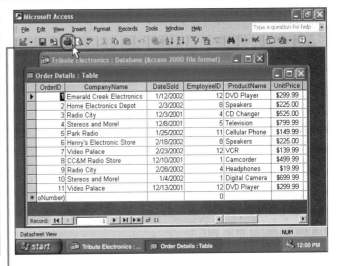

5 Click the print option you want to use (○ changes to ⊙).

Note: For information on the print options, see the top of this page.

■ If you selected **Pages** in step **5**, type the number of the first page you want to print. Press the `Tab` key and then type the number of the last page you want to print.

6 Click **OK**.

QUICKLY PRINT ALL RECORDS

1 Click 🖨 to quickly print all the records.

273

CREATE MAILING LABELS

You can create a
mailing label for
every person in
a table. You can
use mailing labels
for addressing
envelopes and
packages, labeling
file folders and
creating name tags.

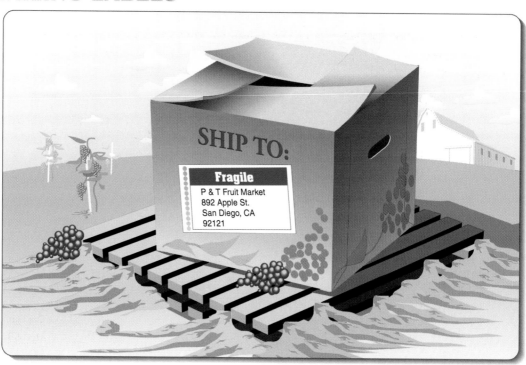

The Label Wizard
asks you a series
of questions and
then creates mailing
labels based on
your answers.

CREATE MAILING LABELS

1 Click **Reports** in
the Database window.

2 Click **New**.

■ The New Report
dialog box appears.

3 Click **Label Wizard**
to use a wizard to create
mailing labels.

4 Click ▼ in this area
to select the table that
contains the information
you want to appear on
the labels.

5 Click the table that
contains the information.

6 Click **OK** to continue.

What information must I specify when creating mailing labels?

When creating mailing labels, you must specify the manufacturer, type and size of labels you want to use.

Manufacturer

You can select from several different label manufacturers, such as Avery, CoStar and Herma.

Label Type

You can choose between sheet feed and continuous labels. Sheet feed labels are individual pages of labels. Continuous labels are connected pages of labels, usually with holes punched along each side.

Label Size

You can select a label size to specify the dimensions of each label and the number of labels that will print across each page.

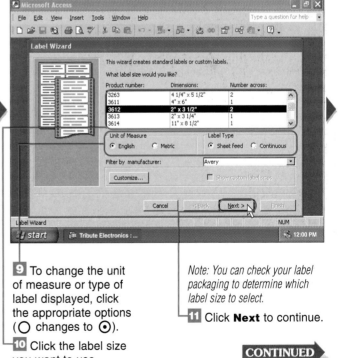

■ The Label Wizard appears.

■ This area displays the available label sizes for the current manufacturer.

7 To display the label sizes for a different manufacturer, click ▾ in this area.

8 Click the manufacturer of the labels you want to use.

9 To change the unit of measure or type of label displayed, click the appropriate options (○ changes to ⊙).

10 Click the label size you want to use.

Note: You can check your label packaging to determine which label size to select.

11 Click **Next** to continue.

CONTINUED

CREATE MAILING LABELS

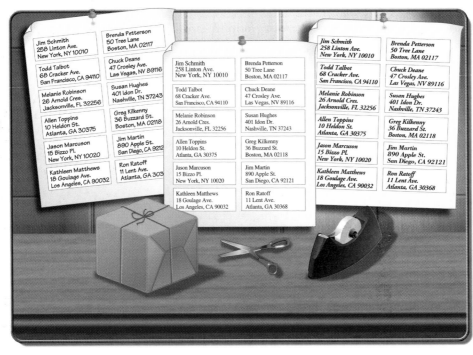

You can change how text will appear on your mailing labels.

The changes you make to the appearance of text on your mailing labels will affect all the text on every label. You cannot change the appearance of text for part of a label or only some labels.

CREATE MAILING LABELS (CONTINUED)

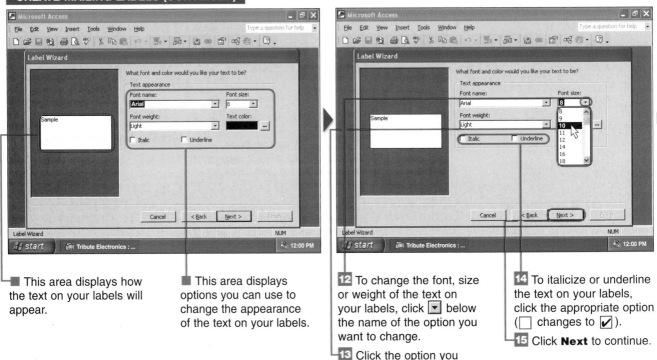

■ This area displays how the text on your labels will appear.

■ This area displays options you can use to change the appearance of the text on your labels.

12 To change the font, size or weight of the text on your labels, click ▼ below the name of the option you want to change.

13 Click the option you want to use.

14 To italicize or underline the text on your labels, click the appropriate option (☐ changes to ☑).

15 Click **Next** to continue.

How can I select a different text color for my mailing labels?

In the Label Wizard, click the button () beside the Text color box. In the dialog box that appears, click the color you want to use for the text and then press the Enter key. You need a color printer to be able to print the text on your mailing labels in color.

Can I display the same text on every mailing label?

Yes. You can display text, such as "Confidential" or "Important", on every mailing label. After you add the fields you want to display on the mailing labels in the Label Wizard, type the text you want to appear on every mailing label in the Prototype label area.

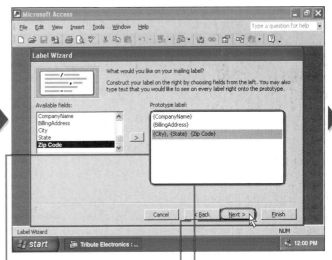

■ This area displays the fields from the table you selected in step **5**.

16 Double-click a field you want to appear on the labels.

■ The field you select appears in this area.

17 To add a blank space, press the **Spacebar**. To move to the next line, press the Enter key.

18 Repeat steps **16** and **17** until this area displays all the fields you want the labels to display.

Note: The fields should appear the same way you want them to print on your labels. Make sure you add spaces and commas (,) where needed.

■ To remove a field you accidentally selected, click the field in this area and then press the Delete key.

19 Click **Next** to continue.

CONTINUED ▶

CREATE MAILING LABELS

You can sort your mailing labels to better organize the labels.

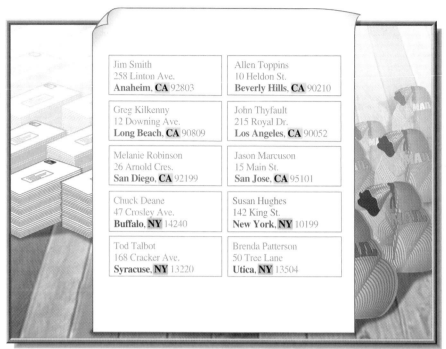

Jim Smith
258 Linton Ave.
Anaheim, CA 92803

Allen Toppins
10 Heldon St.
Beverly Hills, CA 90210

Greg Kilkenny
12 Downing Ave.
Long Beach, CA 90809

John Thyfault
215 Royal Dr.
Los Angeles, CA 90052

Melanie Robinson
26 Arnold Cres.
San Diego, CA 92199

Jason Marcuson
15 Main St.
San Jose, CA 95101

Chuck Deane
47 Crosley Ave.
Buffalo, NY 14240

Susan Hughes
142 King St.
New York, NY 10199

Tod Talbot
168 Cracker Ave.
Syracuse, NY 13220

Brenda Patterson
50 Tree Lane
Utica, NY 13504

For example, you can sort your mailing labels by state to place all the labels for the same state together. If the same state appears on several labels, you can sort your labels by a second field, such as city, to further organize the labels.

CREATE MAILING LABELS (CONTINUED)

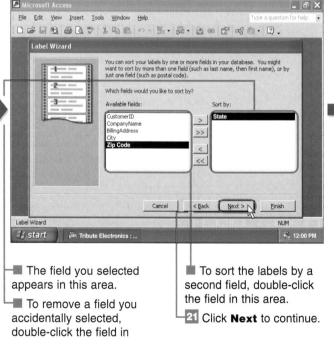

20 To sort your labels, double-click the field you want to use to sort the labels.

Note: If you do not want to sort your labels, skip to step 21.

■ The field you selected appears in this area.

■ To remove a field you accidentally selected, double-click the field in this area.

■ To sort the labels by a second field, double-click the field in this area.

21 Click **Next** to continue.

How do I print the mailing labels I created?

When viewing your mailing labels, click the Print button () to print all the labels. Before printing your mailing labels, make sure your printer is turned on and the labels are in the printer. For more information on printing, see page 272.

How do I edit the mailing labels I created?

To edit mailing labels, you must change the data in the table you used to create the labels. Changes you make to the data in the table will automatically appear in the labels the next time you open the report containing the labels.

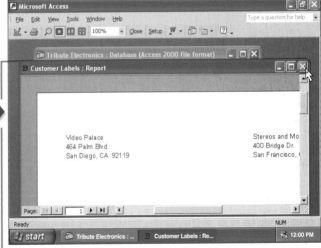

22 Type a name for your labels.

23 Click **Finish** to create your labels.

■ You can click **Back** to return to a previous step and change your selections.

■ A window appears, displaying a personalized label for each person in your table.

24 When you finish reviewing the labels, click ☒ to close the window.

■ Access stores your labels as a report. To later open a report so you can once again review and print your labels, see page 256.

Create Data Access Pages

Are you wondering how you can use Access to share data with other people on the Internet? This chapter shows you how to create and work with data access pages for the Web.

CREATE A DATA ACCESS PAGE

You can use the Page Wizard to create a data access page, which is a Web page that connects directly to the data in your database.

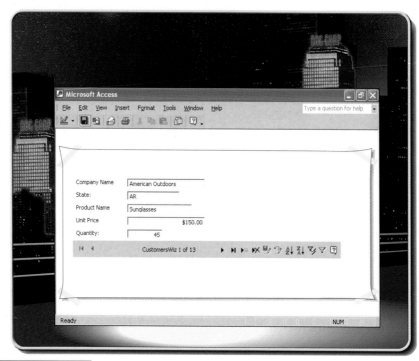

You can use a data access page to view and edit the data in your database on the Internet or your company's intranet. An intranet is a small version of the Internet within a company.

The Page Wizard will ask you a series of questions and then set up a data access page based on your answers.

CREATE A DATA ACCESS PAGE

■ To create a data access page, you must have Internet Explorer 5 or a later version installed on your computer.

1 Click **Pages** in the Database window.

2 Double-click **Create data access page by using wizard**.

■ The Page Wizard appears.

3 To select the table that contains the fields you want to include in your page, click ▼ in this area.

4 Click the table that contains the fields.

Which tables in my database can I use to create a data access page?

You can use any table in your database to create a data access page. When creating a data access page that uses information from more than one table, relationships must exist between the tables so that Access can bring together the information in the tables. For information on relationships, see page 124.

Can I create a data access page using data from a query?

Yes. The Page Wizard allows you to select the fields you want to include from queries as you would select the fields you want to include from tables. For information on queries, see pages 190 to 229.

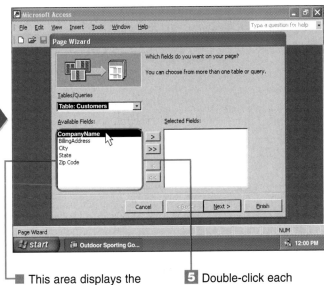

■ This area displays the fields from the table you selected.

5 Double-click each field you want to include in your page.

Note: To add all the fields in the table at once, click `>>` .

■ Each field you select appears in this area.

■ To remove a field you accidentally selected, double-click the field in this area.

Note: To remove all the fields at once, click `<<` .

6 To include fields from other tables in your database, repeat steps **3** to **5** for each table.

7 Click **Next** to continue.

CONTINUED

CREATE A DATA ACCESS PAGE

You can group the data in your data access page to place related information together. Grouping data helps you organize the data in your page.

For example, you can group all the customers from the same state together in your data access page.

■ This area displays all the fields you selected to include in your page.

8 If you want to group data in your page, double-click the field you want to use to group the data.

■ This area shows how Access will group the data in your page.

■ To remove a field you selected to group data in your page, double-click the field in this area.

9 Click **Next** to continue.

10 To sort the records in your page, click ▼ in this area.

Note: For information on sorting, see the top of page 285.

11 Click the field you want to use to sort the records.

Why would I sort the records in my data access page?

You can sort the records in your data access page to better organize the records. For example, you can sort records alphabetically by the Last Name field to make it easier to find customers of interest. If the same last name appears more than once in the field, you can sort records by a second field, such as First Name, to further organize the records. You can use up to four fields to sort the records in a data access page.

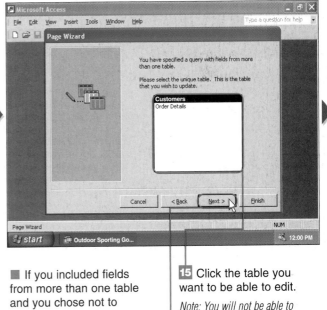

12 Click this button until the button displays the way you want to sort the records.

Ascending—Sorts A to Z, 1 to 9

Descending—Sorts Z to A, 9 to 1

13 To sort by a second field, repeat steps **10** to **12** in this area.

14 Click **Next** to continue.

■ If you included fields from more than one table and you chose not to group data in step **8**, this screen appears.

*Note: If the screen does not appear, skip to step **17**.*

15 Click the table you want to be able to edit.

Note: You will not be able to edit data in the other table(s).

16 Click **Next** to continue.

CONTINUED

285

CREATE A DATA ACCESS PAGE

When creating
a data access
page, you can
give the page
a descriptive
title.

When you view
a data access
page, the title
you specify
will appear at
the top of the
window.

CREATE A DATA ACCESS PAGE (CONTINUED)

17 Type a title for your page.

18 Click this option to open the page when you finish creating the page (○ changes to ◉).

19 Click **Finish** to create your page.

■ You can click **Back** to return to a previous step and change your selections.

■ The page appears, displaying the information for the first record.

Note: To move through records in a data access page, see page 292.

20 Click 🖫 to save your page.

Where does Access store a data access page I create?

Access stores a data access page as a separate file outside of your database and displays a shortcut to the file in the Database window. To use the shortcut to open a data access page within Access, see page 290.

How do I make my data access page available for other people to view?

To make a data access page available on the Internet or your company's intranet, you need to transfer the page to a Web server. A Web server is a computer that stores Web pages and makes the pages available for other people to view. For information on publishing a data access page to a Web server, contact your Web server administrator.

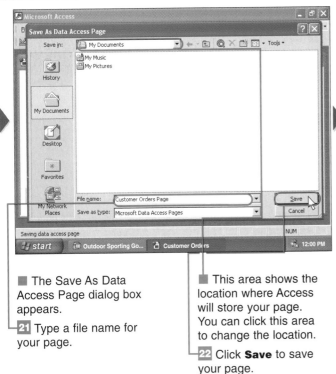

■ The Save As Data Access Page dialog box appears.

21 Type a file name for your page.

■ This area shows the location where Access will store your page. You can click this area to change the location.

22 Click **Save** to save your page.

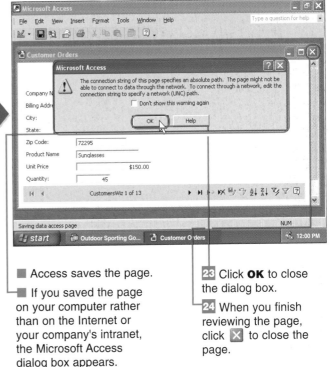

■ Access saves the page.

■ If you saved the page on your computer rather than on the Internet or your company's intranet, the Microsoft Access dialog box appears.

23 Click **OK** to close the dialog box.

24 When you finish reviewing the page, click ✕ to close the page.

CHANGE THE VIEW OF A DATA ACCESS PAGE

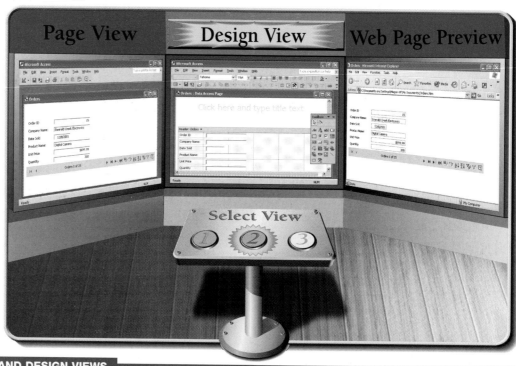

Page View   Design View   Web Page Preview

Select View

① ② ③

You can view a data access page in three different ways. Each view allows you to perform different tasks.

USING THE PAGE AND DESIGN VIEWS

■ In this example, the data access page appears in the Page view.

1 Click to display the data access page in the Design view.

■ The data access page appears in the Design view.

■ The View button changed from to .

■ To quickly switch between the Page () and Design () views, click the View button.

How can I view a data access page?

Design View

The Design view allows you to change the layout and design of a data access page to make the page easier to use or to enhance the appearance of the page.

Page View

The Page view allows you to review, enter and edit information displayed in a data access page.

Web Page Preview

The Web Page Preview view allows you to display a data access page in your Web browser so you can see how the page will appear on the Web or on your company's intranet.

USING THE WEB PAGE PREVIEW VIEW

■ Before you can display your data access page in a Web browser, you must save any changes you made to the page.

1 Click 🖫 to save any changes you made to the data access page.

2 Click ⏷ in this area to display the data access page in a different view.

3 Click **Web Page Preview**.

■ The Microsoft Internet Explorer window appears, displaying the page as it will appear on the Web or on your company's intranet.

4 When you finish reviewing the page, click ✕ to close the page.

OPEN A DATA ACCESS PAGE

You can open a data access page to display the contents of the page on your screen. Opening a data access page allows you to review and make changes to the page.

Each time you open a data access page, Access will display the most current data from your database in the page.

OPEN A DATA ACCESS PAGE

1 Click **Pages** in the Database window.

■ This area displays a list of the data access pages you have created in the database.

2 Double-click the data access page you want to open.

■ The data access page opens. You can now review and make changes to the page.

■ When you finish reviewing and working with the data access page, click ✕ to close the page.

You can add a
title to a data
access page to
describe the
information
displayed in
the page.

ADD A TITLE

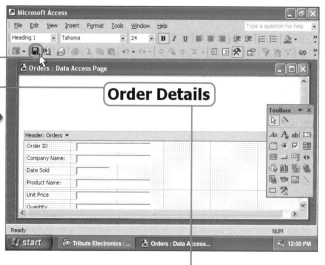

1 Display the data access
page you want to add a title
to in the Design view. To
change the view of a data
access page, see page 288.

2 Click this area to
add a title to the data
access page.

■ A flashing insertion
point appears in the area.

3 Type a title for your
data access page.

4 Click 🔲 to save
your change.

■ To remove a title from
a data access page, drag
the mouse I over the
title until you highlight
the entire title and then
press the Delete key.

MOVE THROUGH RECORDS

You can move through the records in a data access page to review and edit information.

MOVE THROUGH RECORDS

■ This area displays the number of the current record and the total number of records.

1 To move to another record, click one of the following buttons.

|◄| First record

|◄| Previous record

|►| Next record

|►| Last record

■ The information for the record you specified appears.

Can I edit the data in my data access page?

Yes. You can edit the data in a data access page as you would edit data on a form. To edit data on a form, see page 142. After you finish making changes to data, click in the data access page to save your changes. When you change data in a data access page, Access will also change the data in the table you used to create the page.

If your data access page displays information from more than one table, you may not be able to edit data in the page.

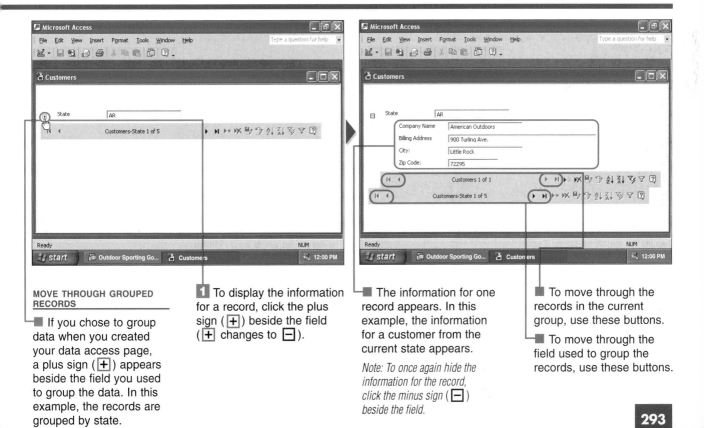

MOVE THROUGH GROUPED RECORDS

■ If you chose to group data when you created your data access page, a plus sign (+) appears beside the field you used to group the data. In this example, the records are grouped by state.

1 To display the information for a record, click the plus sign (+) beside the field (+ changes to −).

■ The information for one record appears. In this example, the information for a customer from the current state appears.

Note: To once again hide the information for the record, click the minus sign (−) beside the field.

■ To move through the records in the current group, use these buttons.

■ To move through the field used to group the records, use these buttons.

APPLY A THEME

Access offers
many ready-to-use
designs, called
themes, that
you can use to
enhance the overall
appearance of a
data access page.

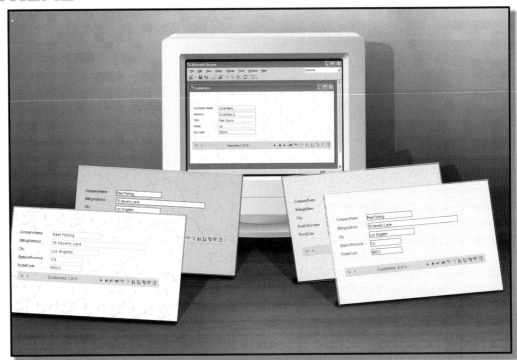

A theme includes
a group of design
elements including
fonts, horizontal lines,
links, bullets and
background pictures.

APPLY A THEME

1 Click **Pages** in the
Database window.

■ This area displays a list
of the data access pages
you have created in the
database.

2 Click the data access
page you want to apply a
theme to.

3 Click **Design** to open
the data access page in
the Design view.

■ The data access page
appears in the Design view.

4 Click **Format**.

5 Click **Theme**.

■ The Theme dialog box
appears.

Why didn't a sample of the theme I selected appear?

If a sample of the theme you selected does not appear, the theme is not installed on your computer. To install the theme, insert the CD you used to install Access into your CD drive and then click **Install** in the Theme dialog box.

Are there other ways I can change the appearance of a data access page?

When you display a data access page in the Design view, you can change the design of the page as you would change the design of a form. For example, you can bold text, change the font and color of text and add a picture to the page. To change the design of a form, see pages 152 to 167.

■ This area displays a list of the available themes.

6 Click the theme you want to apply to your data access page.

■ This area displays a sample of the theme you selected.

Note: If a sample does not appear, see the top of this page.

7 Click **OK** to apply the theme to your data access page.

■ The data access page displays the theme you selected.

8 Click 🖫 to save your change.

■ To remove a theme, repeat steps 1 to 8, selecting **(No Theme)** in step 6.

RENAME A DATA ACCESS PAGE

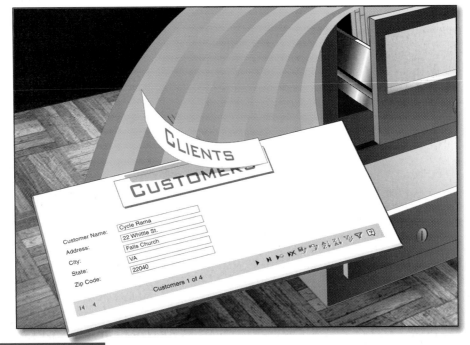

You can change
the name of
a data access
page to better
describe the
information
displayed in
the page.

Each data
access page in
your database
must have a
unique name.

RENAME A DATA ACCESS PAGE

1 Click **Pages** in the
Database window.

■ This area displays a
list of the data access
pages you have created
in the database.

2 Click the name of the
data access page you want
to rename.

3 After a few seconds,
click the name again or press
the F2 key. A black border
appears around the name.

*Note: If you accidentally double-click
the name of the data access page,
the page will open.*

4 Type a new name for
the data access page and
then press the Enter key.

■ The data access page
displays the new name.

*Note: Access stores a data access
page as a separate file outside of
your database. Renaming a data
access page in Access renames
the shortcut to the file, but does
not rename the file itself.*

If you no longer need a data access page, you can permanently delete the page from your database.

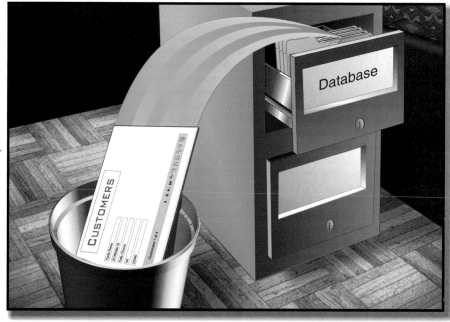

Access stores a data access page as a separate file outside of your database and displays a shortcut to the file in the Database window. When deleting a data access page, you can delete both the shortcut to the file and the file itself or just the shortcut.

DELETE A DATA ACCESS PAGE

1 Click **Pages** in the Database window.

■ This area displays a list of the data access pages you have created in the database.

2 Click the name of the data access page you want to delete.

3 Click ☒ to delete the data access page.

■ A confirmation dialog box appears.

4 Click a button to specify if you want to delete both the shortcut to the file and the file itself or just the shortcut.

*Note: If you select **Delete Link and Files** in step 4, the Confirm File Delete dialog box will appear. Click **Yes** to delete the file.*

INDEX

INDEX

G

INDEX

INDEX

306

with these full-color Visual™ guides